THE GOLF SWING: IT'S ALL IN THE HANDS

The Golf Swing

IT'S ALL IN THE HANDS

James Lythgoe

Printed and bound in Canada.

Library and Archives Canada Cataloguing-in-Publication Data

Lythgoe, James, 1960–
The golf swing: it's all in the hands / James Lythgoe.

ISBN 978-0-9919243-3-2

1. Swing (Golf).
I. Title.

GV979.S9L98 2010 796.352'3
C2010-902264-5

In memory of Al Finnegan, a veteran of the Second World War, who fought in Normandy on D-Day. Sadly, Al passed away on December 24, 2008.

When asked about D-Day, Al spoke first about the unbelievable noise; then he recalled the young French girl he found in a trench, two miles in from the shore. The troops picked her up and took her to the nearest farmhouse. Al often wondered what became of her.

After watching the television broadcast of the ceremonies commemorating the forty-fifth anniversary of D-Day, Al could not sleep for three or four nights – a reminder to us all of the heavy memories war veterans endure. They sacrificed; we benefit. Let us not forget.

Acknowledgements

DOUGLAS CAMPBELL WILLINGLY APPLIED his meticulous command of the English language to my writing. Doug has a special talent for language, and I will be forever grateful to him. Thank you, Doug, you made a contribution to this book I couldn't have made myself.

Working with Suzanne Burkill and Liz Payne was definitely one of the highlights of the experience of producing this book. Suzanne gave very generously of her time as graphic designer, as did Liz in colour-correcting my photographs. Both are highly skilled in their respective fields, and the high quality of their work in this book speaks for itself. Their personal commitment helped me to achieve my goal. I will be forever grateful to Suzanne and Liz for their efforts, and I will never forget the experience of working with them. Thank you both very much.

Lorne Rubenstein of *The Globe and Mail* gave me advice early on in the project. I didn't exactly follow this advice, but I did pursue my goal to its completion. Thank you, Lorne, for your advice and your encouragement. I believe that, subconsciously, it did help me to complete this book.

Greg N. Dukart granted me permission to shoot the photographs for this book at The Links at Crowbush Cove (www.golflinkspei.com). Recognized by *Golf Digest* as the Best New Course in 1994, The Links at Crowbush Cove is situated around the dunes on the north shore of PEI near Morell, about a thirty-minute drive from Charlottetown. Thank you, Greg, for granting me permission, and thank you to the kind staff of The Links at Crowbush Cove.

John Macleod of Stratford, Prince Edward Island, as is typical of all Islanders, freely offered me his help and hospitality. Thank you, John.

My father and my sister, Dr. Colin Lythgoe and Catherine, respectively, helped in ways only family can. Your early morning help with the photographs is greatly appreciated. Thank you.

A special thanks to Maggie McPhail, Eric Stewart, Linda Jenkins, Kevin Gardiner, and Garry Black for all your kind assistance.

I would like to acknowledge the expert golf instruction to be found in the books I cite: *Jack Nicklaus' Lesson Tee*; Ben Hogan's *Five Lessons: The Modern Fundamentals of Golf*; and Paul Runyan's *The Short Way to Lower Scoring*. Thanks also to the late Moe Norman, who demonstrated to us all that the impossible is possible: that you can hit the ball purely and accurately three hundred and sixty-five days a year!

Contents

Introduction: Waving at the Golf Ball

BY FAR THE MOST IMPORTANT factor in the achievement of an effective golf swing is the correct use of the hands. Without a conscious awareness of how your hands are operating, you will always feel that your swing lacks something. In my thirty years of golfing, I have never known of anyone giving lessons on the use of the hands. This is why I have written this book.

One morning during the 1987 Qualifying School for the Canadian Tour, I was having my breakfast at the club and noticed Moe Norman, the best ball striker golf has ever seen, sitting at a table next to me. Knowing Moe's reputation for being shy with strangers, I resisted the impulse to say hello. Later that day I saw a large gallery gathered on the practice tee, and decided to go over and have a look. Moe was putting on a show for an audience that was in awe of his swing. As he demonstrated his skill, Moe remarked to the gallery that the mistake many golfers make is to "wave" at the ball. Moe was referring to the hand action of the amateur golfer, and what he said confirmed my observations exactly.

The correct hand action is very deliberate and precise. There is no room for error. This book explains that action in detail, and, since it is impossible to use the correct hand action during the swing unless the shoulders are also moving properly, Chapter 4 provides a short lesson on how to coordinate your shoulders with your hands. My intention is to give golfers the lessons they need in order to eliminate the hand waving that the late Moe Norman and I observed.

When you hit a golf shot, the only link between you and the ball is the club, so you want this link to be as good as it can be. To achieve this, you need proper hand action, and your body needs to move in a manner consistent with your hands. Once you know how to establish these conditions you are on your way to becoming a good golfer. The golf swing is not particularly difficult to develop when you know the hand action, but without it the struggle can last forever.

I know from my own experience how fundamental hand action is to the proper motion of the swing: once I had learned how to use my hands and could coordinate the turn of my shoulders with my hand action, I was able to play New Brunswick's Mactaquac Provincial Park golf course, a course of more than 7,000 yards, from the professional tees – and break par.

Many golfers think the grip is the most important element of a good swing. I disagree. There are many golfers who have wonderful grips, but because they use poor hand action they are unable to hit the ball effectively. I have never seen someone with poor hand action produce excellent shots. On the other hand, there have been a few cases of touring professionals who have been able to produce excellent shots *in spite of a poor grip*, because they knew how to use their hands. A good grip is important, but correct hand action is paramount.

The hand action of the swing is best learned from the address position. When you know how to grip the club (as discussed in Chapter 1), and address the ball (Chapter 2), you are ready to take the lesson on hand action (Chapter 3). The lesson itself is not difficult to understand or to learn, but it is subtle in its correctness, so it is necessary to pay close attention to the details and move your hands accordingly.

For over thirty years I have been looking for an explicit explanation of the subject, but I have never been able to find one. It simply doesn't exist in the golf literature. This is not to suggest that the literature is inadequate. Many aspects of the golf swing are covered thoroughly, and as a whole the literature provides excellent instruction. This book is simply intended to fill a small but vital gap.

There are a couple of things I would like to point out about the book. First, please note that since I am right-handed, the instructions and photographs provided here assume that you are right-handed too. If you are left-handed, the text and photographs will still be valuable to you – just substitute "left" for all references to "right," and vice versa. You will also notice that the text appears to be directed to a male reader – I have not used "he/she" and "him/her." I have avoided this because it makes the text confusing and cumbersome. But I am in no way implying that these instructions apply to male golfers only. Female golfers will benefit just as much from these instructions, and I trust they will forgive the stylistic sexism.

I call this book "The Golf Swing: It's All in the Hands" to reflect the fact that the hands dictate how the body moves during the swing. I hope that it helps you improve your swing and lower your score. Enjoy the lessons.

1 | The Golf Grip

Placement of Your Left Hand

THE LOGICAL PLACE TO BEGIN the lesson is the left hand, since that's the first hand you place on the club. The left-hand grip is a palm grip – the club is held in the palm of the hand. The fingers wrap around the club, and the flesh of the palm creates a vice-like grip that prevents the club from turning in your hands at the moment of impact. The forefathers of the modern golf swing developed this excellent grip, and I cannot imagine how I could improve it.

FEATURES OF THE LEFT HAND

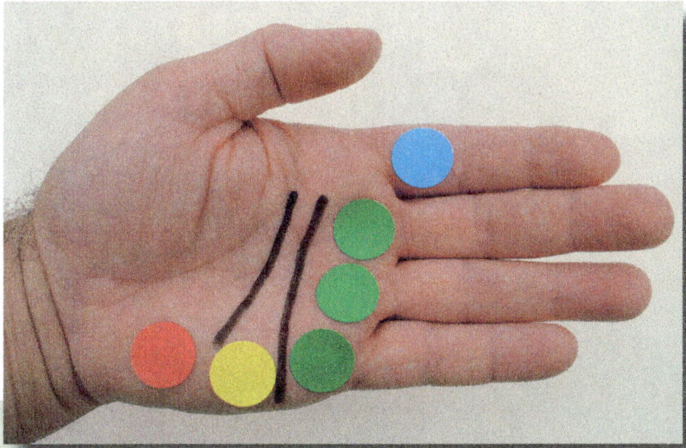

1.00

Areas of the palm of the left hand.

Photograph **1.00** highlights two wrinkles in the palm of the left hand, one of which is shorter than the other. The shorter wrinkle, which stops about three quarters of an inch from the edge of the hand, divides the palm into two fleshy areas, marked, respectively, by a red dot and a yellow dot. The longer wrinkle, which extends to the edge of the hand, defines the boundary between the yellow-dot area and the area of flesh identified by three green dots. Learning how to use these areas of flesh to hold a golf club is a big part of learning the left-hand grip. The areas of flesh identified, respectively, by the red dot and the green dot pinch the club with equal but opposite forces. An imaginary line joining the yellow dot and the blue dot marks where the club crosses the palm of the hand. We have, of course, in addition to these coloured-dot areas, four fingers and a thumb that play roles in forming the left-hand grip.

PLACING A CLUB IN YOUR PALM

Normally, you will begin to assume your grip with the clubhead resting on the ground behind the ball. Keep in mind the position of the clubface relative to your hands, because you do not want it to change when you take your grip. For now I will focus on the features of the left hand and how to use them. Later, I will show you how to keep the clubface in the correct position.

Place the club in your palm

1. Select a flat surface such as a tabletop. Place the clubhead on it with the leading edge of the clubface lying flat on the surface (see photograph **1.01**).

1.01

The clubface lies flat on the coffee table while I slide my hand under the club.

2. Turn your left palm so that it faces upward, and slide it under the club. Position the club across the yellow and blue dots that are marked in photograph **1.00**. Notice that the width of the club prevents the yellow-dot flesh from being pinched; the club presses against the yellow-dot flesh and compresses it (see photograph **1.02**). I like to think of the yellow-dot flesh as the bottom of a canyon of flesh, the sides of which are the red-dot flesh and the green-dot flesh. When the club is placed across the yellow dot and the blue dot, you should be able to see the red dot and roughly one and a half green dots (see photograph **1.03**).

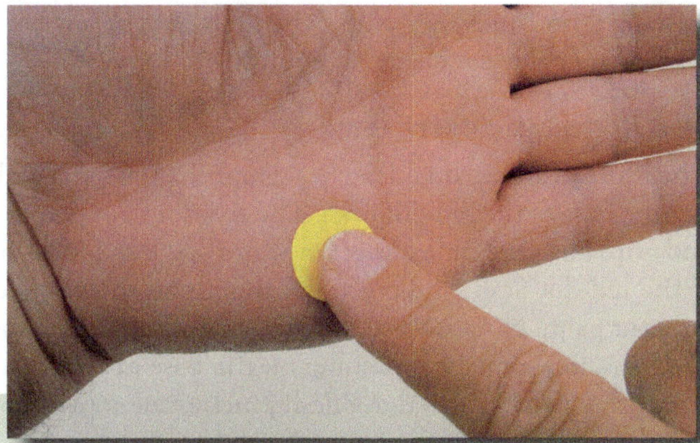

1.02

By pushing down on the yellow dot with my finger I simulate the action of the club, which compresses the yellow-dot flesh rather than pinching it.

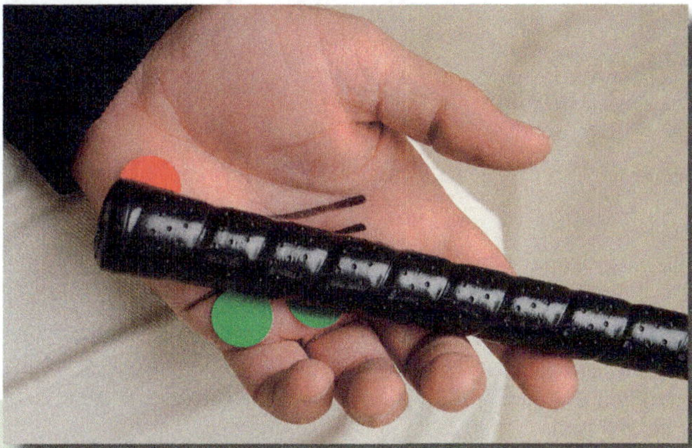

1.03

When the club is positioned across the yellow and blue dots correctly, the red dot and about one and a half green dots are visible.

3. Try wrapping your last three fingers around the club. When you do, the green-dot flesh will squeeze against the underside of the club. If this feels uncomfortable, adjust the club and the flesh until the discomfort disappears. Do you sense that the club is cradled at the bottom of the "canyon of flesh"?

BE CAREFUL – blisters form very easily when the green-dot flesh is squeezed against the club. They have a nasty habit of developing quietly until it is too late. Once a blister has formed in the green-dot area you can be set back a couple of days while it heals. Practise your grip for ten minutes at a time, twice a day, until your flesh toughens up; it may form calluses. Monitor the flesh in your left hand closely as you practise, and if you believe a blister is beginning to form, stop.

A CLOSER LOOK AT THE RED-DOT FLESH

Imagine that the short wrinkle marked in photograph **1.00** is extended to the edge of your hand, at the base of the red-dot flesh. The red-dot flesh plays a critical role in the left-hand grip. Push the index finger of your right hand into your left palm at the base of the red-dot flesh, and place the thumb on the wrinkle separating your wrist from your palm. Now squeeze the red-dot flesh, as in photograph **1.04**, so that the tip of the index finger is pushing on the base of the red-dot flesh. In the left-hand grip, the base of the red-dot flesh pinches the top of the club, while the green-dot flesh pinches the underside of the club.

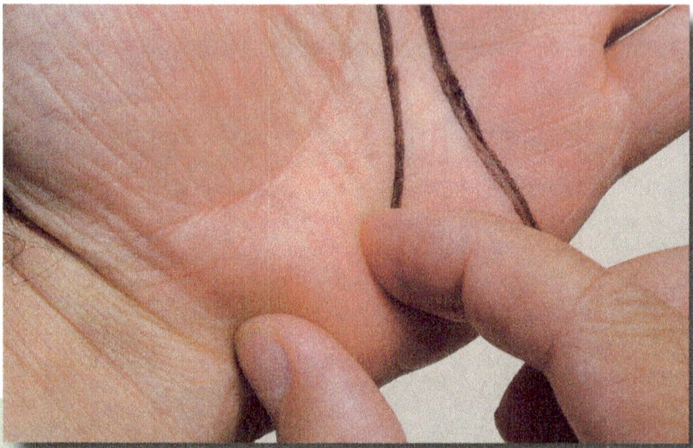

1.04

Squeezing the red-dot flesh between the index finger and the thumb simulates what happens when you grip the club. The base of the red-dot flesh, where the index finger is shown, presses upon the top of the golf club.

THE RED-DOT FLESH IN COMBINATION WITH THE INDEX FINGER

You can pick up a golf club and hold it using only the red-dot flesh and a hooked index finger. If you learn how to hold a club using only these two contact points, you will have learned a significant aspect of the left-hand grip.

Pick up the club using the red-dot flesh and the index finger

1. Place your club on a table with the leading edge of the clubface lying flat on the surface, as in photograph **1.01**.
2. Rest the back of your left hand on your lap, as in photograph **1.05**.
3. With your palm facing upward, slide your hand under the club.

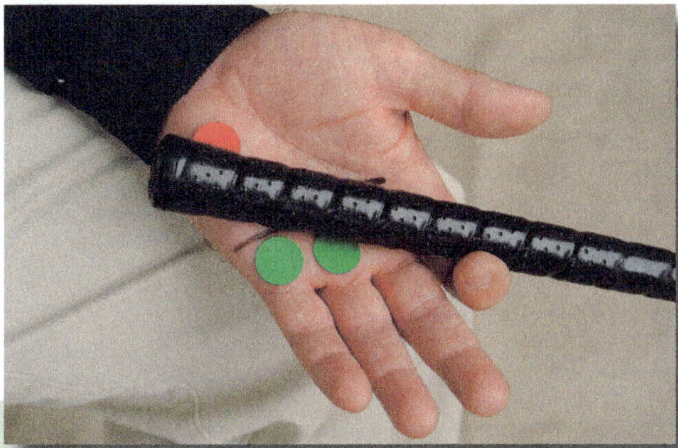

1.05

Place the club across the yellow and blue dots, leaving a quarter of an inch of grip exposed at the end of the club. Hook your index finger around the club.

4. Place the golf club across the yellow and blue dots. Position the base of the red-dot flesh so that it slightly overlaps the top surface of the grip. You may have to push the club into your palm with your right hand in order to do this, as many people do when trying to pinch the grip with the base of the red-dot flesh.
5. Extend the last quarter of an inch of the club beyond the edge of your hand.
6. Hook your index finger around the club, as in photograph **1.05**.
7. Now grasp the end of the club with your right thumb and index finger, as in photograph **1.06**.

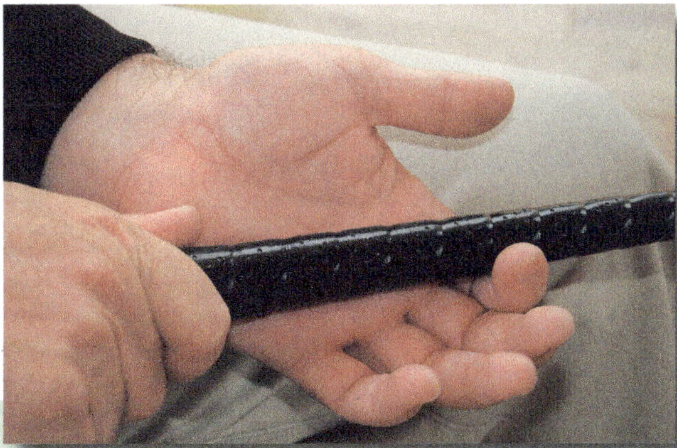

1.06

Grasp the end of the club with the thumb and the index finger of your right hand.

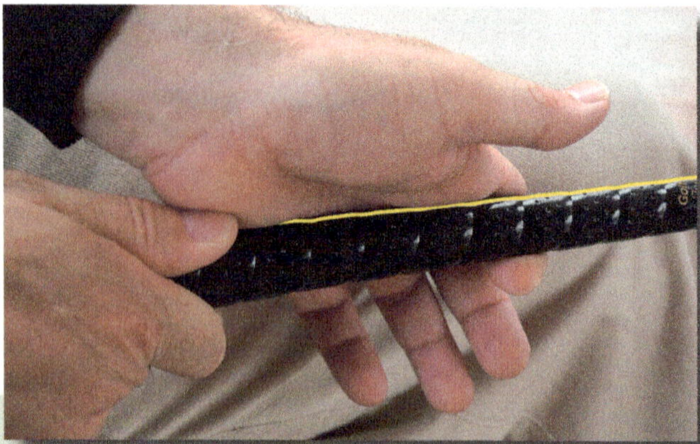

1.07

I rotate my left hand ninety degrees so that it is off my lap. The head of the club follows this movement, and is now perpendicular to the table it originally rested on.

8. Rotate your left hand ninety degrees clockwise so that the back of the left hand is no longer in contact with your lap (photograph **1.07**). Push the club into your palm with your right thumb and index finger as you rotate your left hand. This should prevent the red-dot flesh from sliding off the top of your club. As you rotate your left hand, turn the club with your right thumb and index finger. Stop rotating your left hand when the toe of the clubhead points straight up and the leading edge of the clubface is perpendicular to the surface of the table. If it happens that the base of the red-dot flesh slides off the top of the club while you rotate your left hand, reposition the club in your hand.

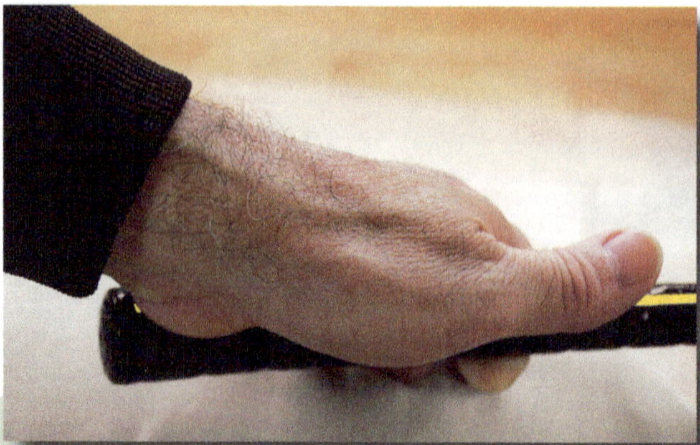

1.08

After I've rotated my left hand ninety degrees, the red-dot flesh is properly positioned on top of the golf club.

9. Before removing your right thumb and index finger from their support of the club, check that the red-dot flesh is on top of it (photograph **1.08**). If you think you need more of the red-dot flesh on top of the club, adjust your left hand accordingly. When you feel confident, try picking up the club from the tabletop using only the red-dot flesh and the index finger (photograph **1.09**). Can you hold the club parallel to the ground with confidence? (It takes a little practice, but because you don't need much room to do this exercise, you can practise it anywhere.) Once you can do this, you will know how the index finger and the red-dot flesh interact with each other.

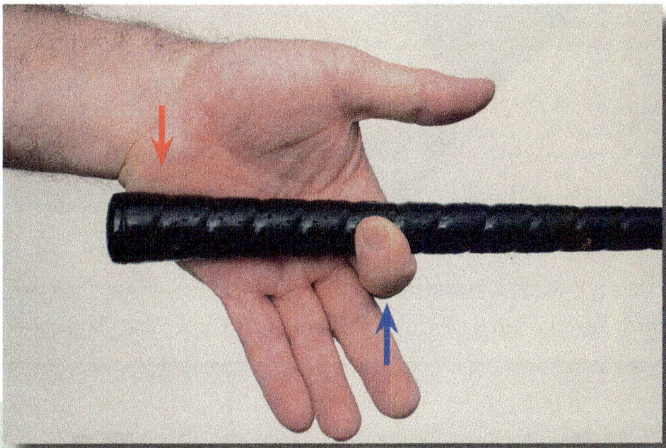

1.09

You can pick up the club and hold it parallel to the ground using only two points of contact. The red-dot flesh applies a downward pressure (the red arrow), which is offset by the upward force applied by the hooked index finger (the blue arrow).

WRAPPING THE LAST THREE FINGERS AROUND THE CLUB

Holding the club securely by the index finger and the red-dot flesh, wrap your last three fingers around it. To make it easier, support the club with your right hand (photograph **1.10**). If the green-dot flesh feels uncomfortable when you wrap your fingers around the club, stop what you are doing, unwrap the last three fingers, and reposition the club in your palm. Try wrapping your last three fingers around the golf club again. The green-dot flesh should squeeze comfortably against the club as your fingers wrap around it.

CLOSE THE GAP

Before placing your left thumb on the club, close the gap between your thumb and your index finger (photograph **1.11**). Then rotate your hand slightly to your right, so that the left side of your thumb contacts the top of the club to the right of centre (photograph **1.12**). If your hand is in the proper position, you should be able to see two knuckles. For myself, I can see the knuckle of the index finger, that of the middle finger, and part of a third knuckle, as shown in photograph **1.12**. This is an acceptable position.

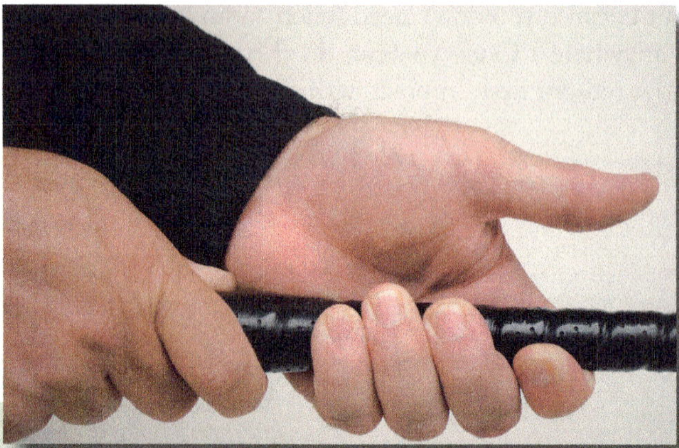

1.10

Wrap the last three fingers around the club while comfortably squeezing the green-dot flesh.

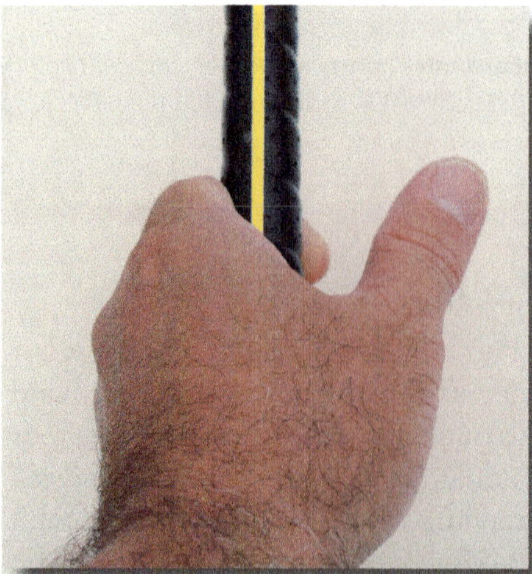

1.11

Close this gap between your left thumb and your index finger before placing the pad of your thumb on the club.

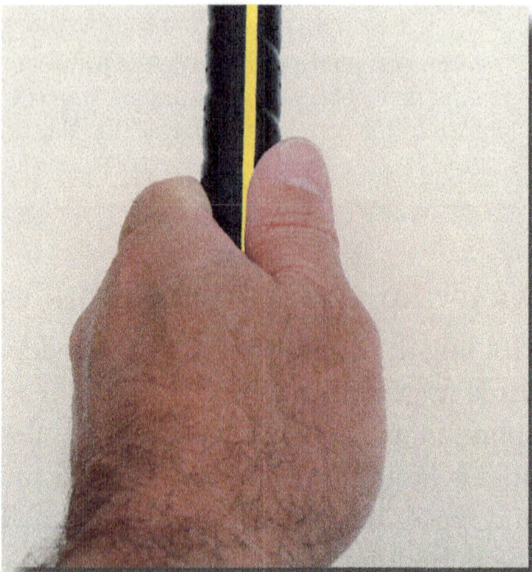

1.12

When the gap is closed, rotate your hand slightly to the right, so that the left thumb contacts the club to the right of centre.

VISE-LIKE GRIP

The red-dot flesh pinches the club from above; the green-dot flesh in combination with the last three fingers pinches the club from below. These two opposing forces create a vise-like grip (photograph **1.13**) that prevents the club from turning in your hands when you hit the ball, as long as the sweet spots of the golf ball and the clubface are aligned at the moment of impact, as in photograph **1.14**. However, if contact occurs toward the toe of the clubface, as in photograph **1.15**, the club will turn in your hands no matter how tightly you grip it. No grip is strong enough to overcome the forces that result from this type of hit.

1.13

A vise-like grip is created when the red-dot flesh presses the club from above while the green-dot flesh and the last three fingers press from below.

1.14

If the sweet spots are aligned at the moment of impact, it is unlikely that the clubhead will turn in your hands. The sweet spot of any clubhead is usually closer to the hosel than to the toe.

1.15

If you contact the ball near the toe of the clubface, it is guaranteed that the club will turn in your hands – an outcome that, of course, you want to avoid.

WHERE TO PLACE YOUR LEFT HAND ON THE CLUB GRIP

As you can see in photograph **1.16**, I leave some open space at the end of the club. Most golf clubs have a white ring or some other mark a quarter of an inch from the end to indicate the point beyond which your left hand should not extend. If you place your left hand too close to the end of the club, as in photograph **1.17**, it is very easy for the last three fingers to slide off. Losing your grip during your swing spells disaster. Most professional golfers leave the quarter-inch margin, and you would be wise to do the same.

LET'S QUICKLY REVIEW the placement of the left hand before seeing how the right hand holds the club. The club should be placed diagonally across the palm and

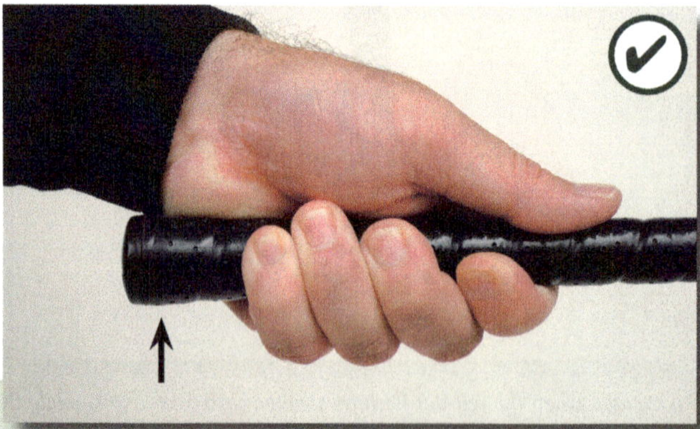

1.16

Position your left hand a quarter-inch from the end of your club.

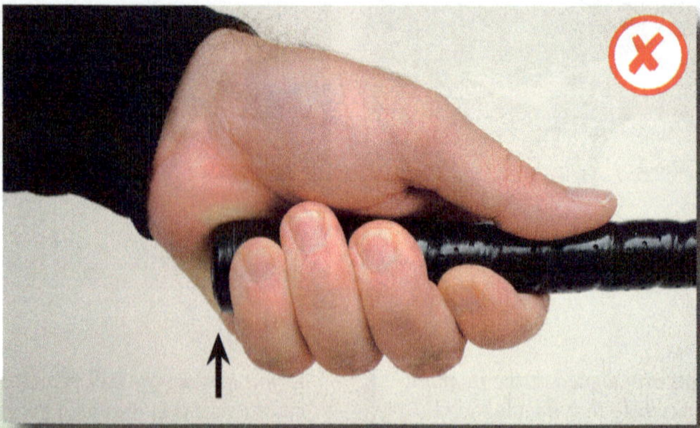

1.17

An incorrect grip. Chances are you will lose your grip on the club during your swing if you hold it this way. For the safety of your foursome, avoid it!

index finger of the left hand – that is, across the yellow and blue dots. Leave a quarter of an inch at the end of the club uncovered by the hand. In this position, the red-dot and green-dot flesh can pinch the club from above and below with a vise-like grip. The thumb should touch the hand, closing the gap between it and the index finger. The thumb should be positioned to the right of the centre of the club. If you wrap the last three fingers around the club and use the flesh of the palm, you should be able to squeeze the club comfortably. If it is not comfortable, begin your grip again. You should be able to see no more than two and a half knuckles, and the clubface should be in the same position as it was when you began your grip.

Now that your left hand is in the correct position, let's turn our attention to the right hand and see how it holds the club.

Placement of the Right Hand

A FINGER GRIP RATHER THAN A PALM GRIP

WE HAVE SEEN THAT the left-hand grip is a palm grip, and that its main purpose is to prevent the club from turning in the hands at the moment of impact. The flesh of the palm forms a vise-like grip. The right-hand grip, however, is a finger grip, not a palm grip.

The right hand is the hitting hand of the golf swing. When the club connects with the ball, it is the right hand that transfers to the club and the ball the energy created by the swing. The right hand moves with speed and precision; thus, it is a finger grip.

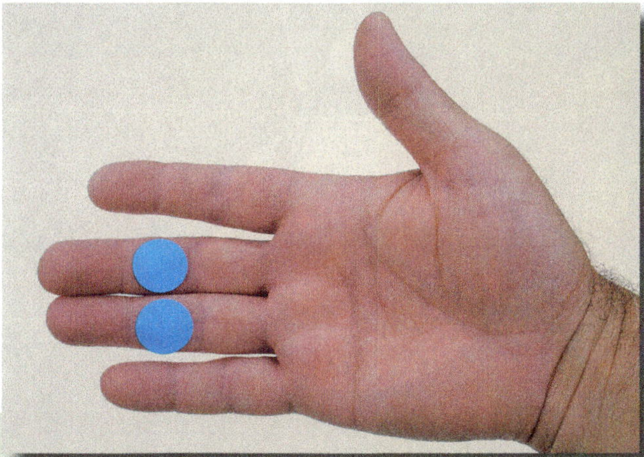

1.18

Anchor these two finger segments to the club before you wrap your right hand around it.

The two blue dots shown in photograph **1.18** identify the areas of the right hand that will make the initial contact with the club. Because you are holding the club in your fingers, you will have a lot more hand to wrap around the club than you had with your left hand. It is therefore very important to learn where, on the underside of the club, you must make the initial contact; if you do not, your hand will finish in the wrong position, and you will have to start over.

Use a Clock Analogy

FIRST, I USE THE IMAGE of a clock to indicate how you should position the club when you are establishing your right-hand grip. Photograph **1.19** shows a clock and a golf ball lying flat on the ground. The leading edge of the clubface is parallel to a line joining twelve o'clock and six o'clock, and this is the position in which your left hand should be holding the club before you place your right hand on it.

I also use the image of a clock to indicate where your right-hand fingers should make their initial contact with the club. Notice that in photograph **1.19** there is a yellow stripe on the top surface of the club. This "top" position represents twelve o'clock on the club. Thus, six o'clock is on the underside of the club, directly opposite the yellow stripe. In the instructions that follow, I will use positions on the clock face to indicate initial points of contact between my fingers and the golf club.

In the photograph, the hand of the clock, which is at six, indicates the initial contact point between my two middle fingers and the club in my first example.

1.19

When the leading edge of the clubface is in line with twelve o'clock and six o'clock, the yellow stripe represents twelve o'clock, and six o'clock is on the side directly opposite.

EXAMPLE ONE: THE SIX O'CLOCK CONTACT POINT (AN INCORRECT POSITION)

Let's see what happens when I take a right-hand grip using the *wrong* starting position. With my left hand in its proper position, I let the ground take the weight of the club, and slide my right fingers under the club until the blue-dot segments of my middle fingers (see photograph **1.18**) contact six o'clock on the underside of the club. My right little finger overlaps my left index finger. (This is explained in more detail later in this chapter.)

I anchor my two middle fingers to the club at six o'clock, as in photograph **1.20**, and then I begin to wrap my right hand over my left thumb, as in photograph **1.21**.

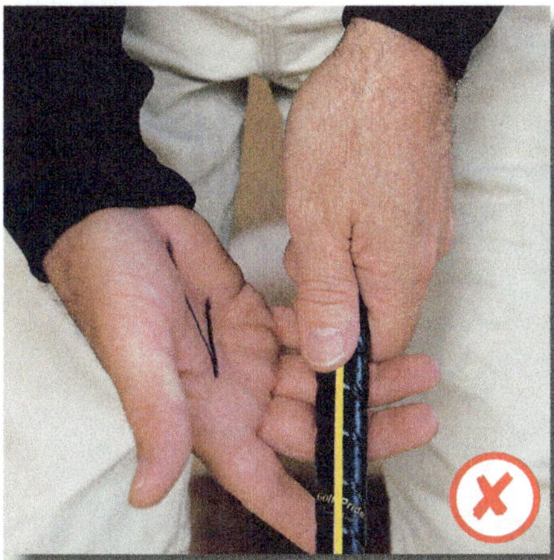

1.20 - *The six o'clock starting point for the right-hand grip.*

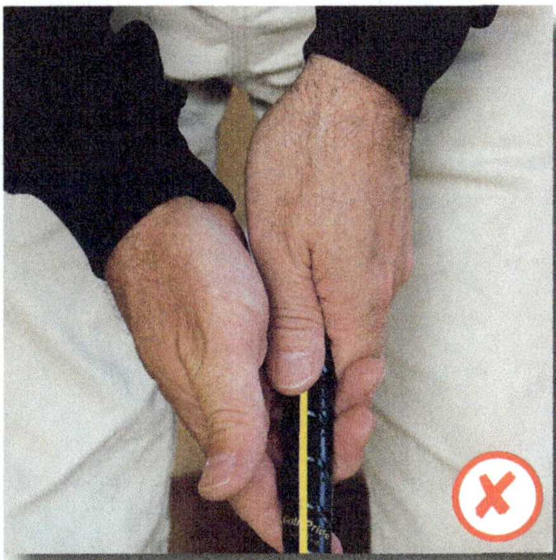

1.21 - *My right hand beginning to wrap over my left thumb.*

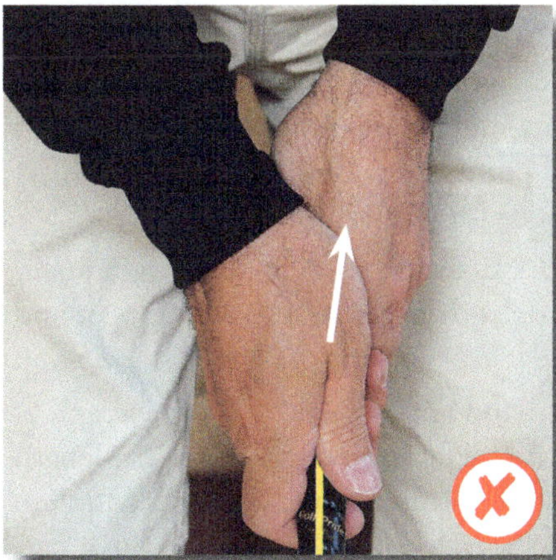

1.22

My right hand finished too far to my left – too much on top of the club. The line formed by my right thumb and my index finger is pointing to the left of my chin, whereas it should point at my chin, or slightly to the right of my chin.

As I continue to wrap my hand around the club, I close the gap between my right thumb and my right index finger. My right thumb contacts the club to the left of centre. The arrow in photograph **1.22** shows that when I do this, the line between my right thumb and my index finger points to the left of my chin. This is a clear sign that my right hand has finished too far to my left and too much on top of the club, and that I will have to do my right-hand grip again, starting from a different position.

EXAMPLE TWO: THE SEVEN O'CLOCK CONTACT POINT (A CORRECT POSITION)

Now I'll use seven o'clock for my initial contact point instead of six o'clock. The minute hand on the clock in photograph **1.23** shows where on the club I will make initial contact.

1.23

The seven o'clock starting position. I have to slide my right hand farther under the club to get to seven o'clock than I did to get to six o'clock. My right hand will finish in a better position this time.

To reach seven o'clock, I have to slide my hand farther under the club (photograph **1.24**). This will alter the final position of my hand. This time, the line between my right thumb and my index finger should point at my chin or at my right eye. Both of these are acceptable finishing positions for the right hand.

I anchor my two middle fingers at seven o'clock. I then wrap my right hand over my left thumb. I close the gap between my right thumb and my index finger and contact the club with my right thumb to the left of centre (photograph **1.25**).

The seven o'clock starting point for my right-hand grip is ideal, given the length of my fingers. You may have to adjust your initial contact point, depending on the length of your fingers and your palm. Find your own best starting point by experimentation.

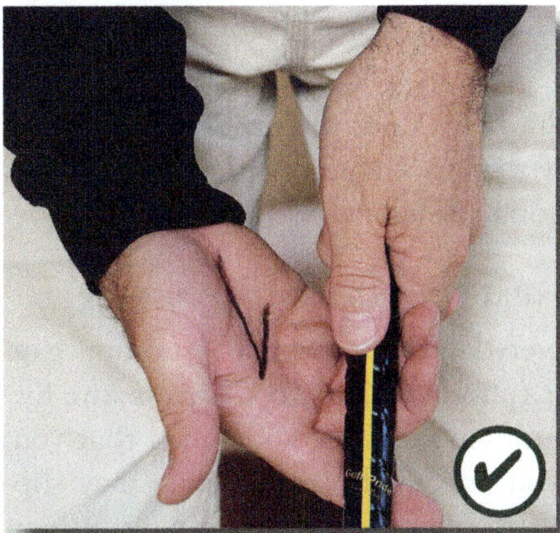

1.24 - *Sliding my right hand farther under the golf club to get to the seven-o'clock position.*

1.25 - *If I use a seven-o'clock starting position, the line between my right thumb and the index finger of my right hand will point exactly where it should – at my chin.*

Two Wrinkles that Form a Letter V

IN PHOTOGRAPH **1.26** two wrinkles in the palm of the right hand are highlighted. These wrinkles intersect to form a letter V. They mark the approximate location where the right hand meets the left thumb when the right hand is wrapped around the club.

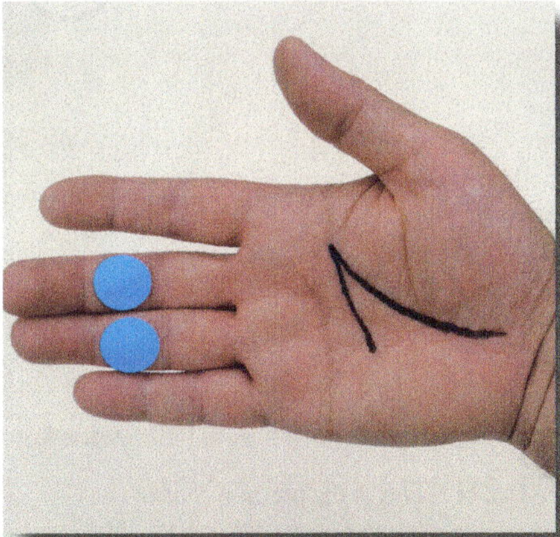

1.26 - *The V of the right palm.*

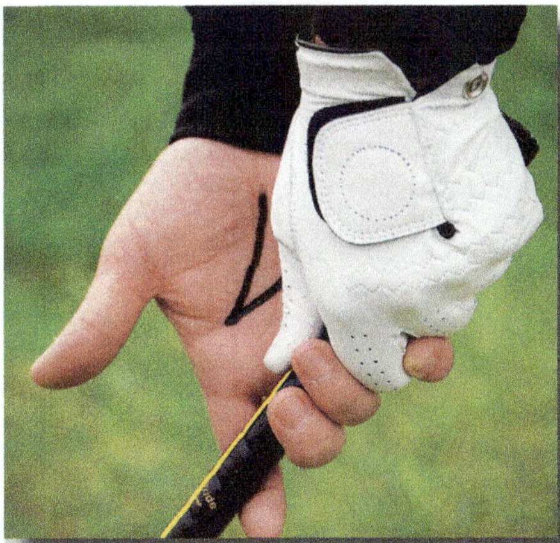

1.27 - *The right hand about to cover the left thumb.*

Photograph **1.27** shows the tip of the left thumb aligned with the vertex of the V of the right palm.

Covering the left thumb with the right palm helps to create unity between the two hands. Note that it is in order to be able to place the right palm over the left thumb that you always place your left hand on the club first.

The Gap Between Your Right Thumb and Your Index Finger

WHEN YOU USE YOUR HANDS to perform everyday tasks, there is a natural gap between your thumb and your index finger (photograph **1.28**). This is fine for doing daily chores, but when you swing a golf club it is recommended that you close the gap, as in photograph **1.29**. If you do not do so, the club may slip between your thumb and your index finger at the top of your backswing. When this happens you will lose control of the club, your downswing will exhibit various faults, and your chances of hitting a good shot are gone. Consciously practise closing the gap during your normal day so that you get used to closing it for your golf grip.

WHEN TO CLOSE THE GAP

When I slide the fingers of my right hand underneath the club shaft, the gap between my index finger and thumb is open, as in photograph **1.30**. At this stage of the grip my main concern is positioning my middle fingers correctly. Whether the gap is open or closed is irrelevant to what I am doing.

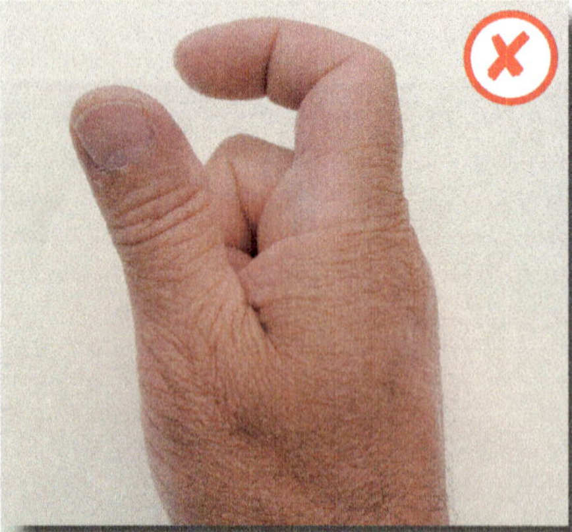

1.28 - *The right hand in its natural position.*

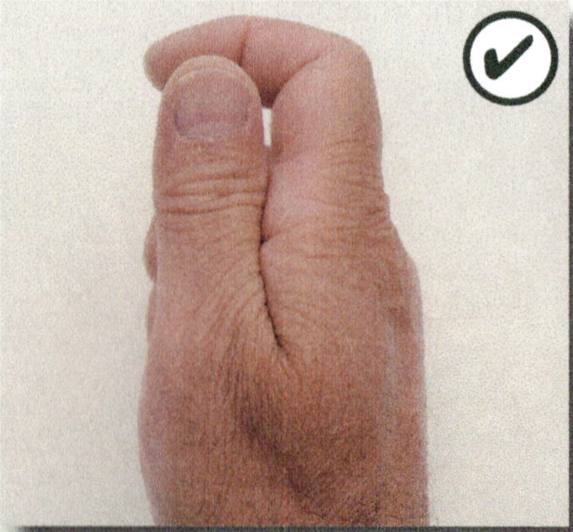

1.29 - *This is the position that is recommended, in order to prevent the club from sliding between your thumb and your index finger at the top of your backswing.*

1.30 - *An open gap at this stage does not matter.*

1.31 - *The right hand is wrapped around the club before it is placed over the left thumb.*

Once I have placed my right hand over my left thumb, as in photographs **1.31** and **1.32**, I am in the final stages of the right-hand grip.

I finish wrapping my right hand around the club, and close the gap. My right thumb then descends to contact the club to the left of centre, as in photograph **1.33**.

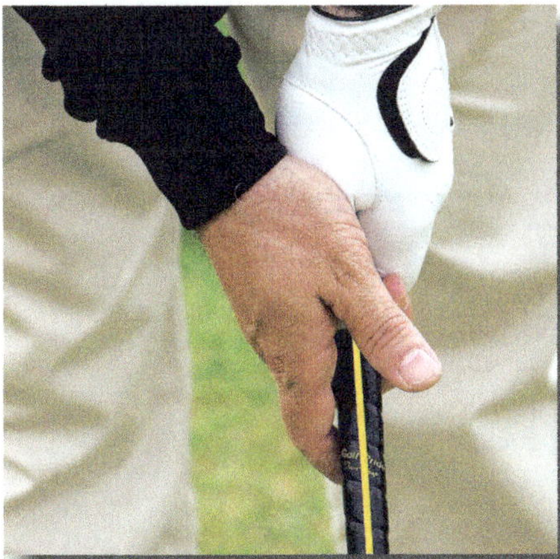

1.32 - *Once the palm of your right hand overlaps your left thumb, start to close the gap between your right thumb and your index finger.*

1.33 - *Place the pad of your right thumb on the club to the left of centre.*

Only Half of Each Thumb Contacts the Club

SINCE YOUR THUMB PADS are flat, and the cross section of the club shaft is round, at first when you place your hands on the club only half of each thumb pad contacts the club. The yellow half-circles in photographs **1.34** and **1.35** indicate those portions of your left thumb pad and your right thumb pad, respectively, that contact the club. In each case, it is the side of the thumb pad that is closest to your palm that contacts the club. However, when your right hand overlaps your left thumb, your left thumb pad is compressed against the club. This is normal.

Photograph **1.36** shows the portion of the right thumb pad that does not make contact with the club, but extends out beyond it.

1.34

The yellow half-circle indicates the portion of the left thumb pad that contacts the club when you are taking your grip.

1.35

The yellow half-circle indicates the portion of the right thumb pad that contacts the club.

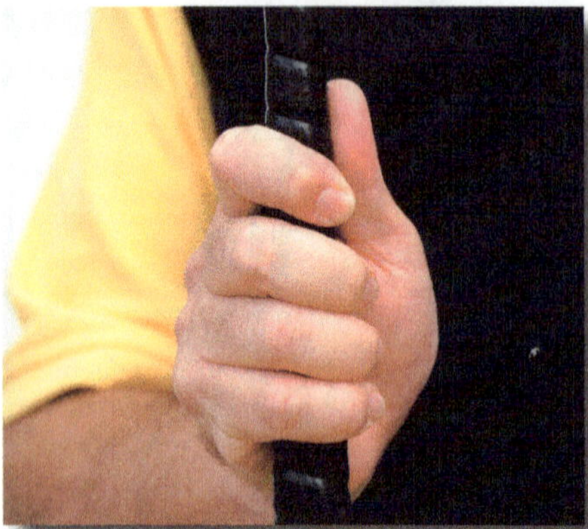

1.36

Half of the right thumb pad does not contact the club.

Gripping the Club

THE HANDS RELATIVE TO THE CLUBFACE

If, as will usually be the case, you wish to strike the ball so that it heads directly to your target, the clubface must be perpendicular to the intended direction of the ball at the moment of impact (see photographs 1.37 and 1.38).

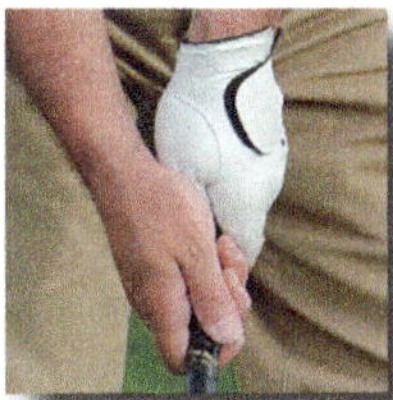

1.37

If the clubface is perpendicular to the intended direction of the ball at the moment of impact, the shot will be straight.

Notice that in this position the clubface forms a ninety-degree angle with the target line. A blow to the ball in the direction of your target with the clubface in this position will produce a shot that flies straight toward your target.

1.38

A view of the clubface when it is perpendicular to the target line.

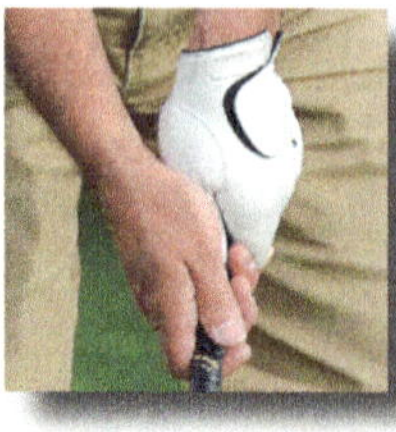

1.39

When the clubface is open at the moment of impact it produces a fade, or slice.

A clubface that is "open" at the moment of impact is shown in photographs **1.39** and **1.40**. In this position, the clubhead is angled away from the ball, and the clubface forms an angle of more than ninety degrees with the target line. If you strike the ball with the clubface in this "open" position you will produce a fade, or slice; that is, a shot that flies off to the right of your target line. Photographs **1.41** and **1.42** show a "closed" clubface at the moment of impact. In this position, the clubhead is angled toward the ball, and the clubface forms an angle of less than ninety degrees with the target line. Striking the ball with the clubface in this "closed" position produces a draw, or hook – a shot that flies off to the left

1.40

A view of the clubface when it is open to the ball.

1.41

When the clubface is closed at the moment of impact it produces a draw, or hook.

of the target line. When you position your hands in relation to the clubface, you must place the clubface perpendicular to the target line, and you must make a conscious effort not to change this position.

SELECTING A STRAIGHT LINE FOR REFERENCE

The first thing I do when I'm preparing to grip a club is find a straight line on the ground – I call it a reference line – and then I make sure that the leading edge of the clubface is aligned perpendicular to it. At home I look for a floor that's tiled, or has some other covering with plenty of straight lines. The lines between tiles

1.42

A view of the clubface when it is closed to the ball.

are ideal for aligning the clubface. If you cannot find a floor covering that has straight lines, use the wall as a reference (see photograph **1.43**), or place a second club on the ground or the floor (photograph **1.44**).

The only catch with using a golf club as a reference line is that the shaft is tapered, so be careful to use the side of the shaft that is closest to you and ignore the other side. Place the reference club far enough away from the ball that you don't hit it with the club you are holding.

1.43

Using the wall as a straight-line reference. Be careful to keep the toe of the club away from the wall.

1.44

Using a golf club or a straight line on the carpet as a reference.

Place the clubface perpendicular to the reference line

1. With your right hand, hold the club partway down on the golf club grip. Leave enough room to allow you to place your left hand close to the end of the club (photograph **1.45**).
2. Let the floor or ground take the full weight of the club.

1.45

Hold the club in your right hand and position the clubface perpendicular to the target line.

3. Position the clubface perpendicular to your chosen reference line (in photograph **1.46**, the tee on the ground, which is aligned with the centre of the ball, forms the reference line). This is exactly what you need in order to hit a straight shot.

Place the club diagonally across the left hand

1. Still holding the club with your right hand, turn your left palm upward, with your fingers fully extended. This allows you to see your left palm so that you

1.46

The clubface is perpendicular to the reference line.

can position the club in it properly. As you become more familiar with the proper grip, you'll probably sense the proper position without needing to see it. For now, though, use your eyes, to make sure you are positioning the club in your left hand correctly.

2. Slide your left hand under the club and place the club across the yellow- and blue-dot areas (photograph **1.47**). This is the starting position for the left-hand grip.
3. Hook your left index finger around the club. Adjust the top of the grip so that it is at the base of the red-dot flesh. Do not press the club against your left palm – you don't want the base of the red-dot flesh to pinch the top of the club grip (see photograph **1.48**). In a few minutes, you will rotate your left hand toward your right. If you pinch the club with the red-dot flesh now, you will find it difficult to rotate your hand. You will pinch the club with the base of the red-dot flesh after you've rotated your hand toward the right.
4. Close your left hand slightly, wrapping your last three fingers loosely around the golf club. The green-dot flesh squeezes against the club as you wrap your

1.47

Slide the left hand under the club, positioning the club on the yellow and blue dots. (The dots are not visible in this photograph because I'm wearing a glove.)

1.48

Hook the left index finger around the club and loosely wrap the last three fingers around it. If this causes pain in the green-dot flesh, adjust the position of the club.

1.49

Rotate the left hand around the club clockwise until you can see two or three knuckles.

1.50

Close the gap between the thumb and the index finger of the left hand. Make sure the left thumb is positioned to the right of centre – that is, to the right of the yellow stripe.

fingers around it. Does your hand feel comfortable? If not, adjust the position of the club so that the green-dot flesh is comfortable when it is squeezed. Next, you need to change the position of the left hand by rotating it clockwise (to the right).

Show two or three knuckles of the left hand

1. Maintain contact between your left hand and the club, but don't press too hard, or you won't be able to rotate your hand clockwise. As your left hand slides around the club, maintain the diagonal (yellow dot–blue dot) position of the club in your hand. Stop rotating your left hand when you can see two or three knuckles as you look down at it (see photograph **1.49**). It is your choice how many knuckles you want to be visible. Many novice golfers feel most comfortable when they can see three of their knuckles, while many experienced golfers prefer to be able to see fewer.

   Once your left hand is in this position, assess whether the club has shifted away from the base of your red-dot flesh. If this has happened, as it often does, now is the time to reposition the club to where it was before you rotated your hand.

1.51

If the left or right thumb is placed off-centre below the highest point of the club, it is difficult for the thumb to slide off it.

1.52

If the left or right thumb sits on top of the club, it is easy for the thumb to slide off it.

2. Pinch the club, using the red-dot flesh, and then lock the last three fingers in place around the club so that the green-dot flesh squeezes comfortably against the club. The green-dot flesh applies an upward force against the underside of the golf club, while the red-dot flesh applies a downward force against the top of the club. These opposite forces create the vice-like grip that prevents the club from turning in your hands at the moment of impact.
3. Close the gap between your left thumb and your index finger, and make sure your left thumb contacts the club to the right of centre, as in photograph **1.50**.

   Positioning the thumb to the right of centre is important, because it places the thumb pad below the highest point of the grip (see photograph **1.51**). This helps prevent the thumb from sliding off the club during the swing.

   To experience the difference in thumb positions, try placing the thumb pad on top of the shaft (see photograph **1.52**), and see how easily it can be dislodged from this position, and then position the thumb correctly, to the right of centre, as shown in photograph **1.51**, and see how difficult it is to dislodge the thumb from the grip.

Joining the Right Hand and the Left Hand

NOW YOU NEED TO KNOW how to join the right hand with the left hand. You have three choices: the overlapping grip, the interlocking grip, and the baseball grip. Essentially, your choice of grip depends on the length of your fingers and your personal preferences.

THE OVERLAPPING GRIP

In the overlapping grip, the right little finger overlaps the left index finger. Many golfers who have long fingers prefer this grip.

Overlap the left index finger with the right little finger

1. Hook the right little finger around the middle joint of the left index finger, as in photograph **1.53**. The right little finger exerts a force on the left index finger, producing a strong connection between the hands. Notice that the middle joint of the left index finger protrudes between the right little finger and the right ring finger. This is the correct way to overlap the hands.
2. Push the right ring finger snugly up against the left index finger. You want the connection between the hands to be as solid as possible.
3. Photograph **1.54** shows an incorrect version of the overlapping grip. Do not place the right little finger over the left index finger joint for joint as we see in this photograph. Doing so creates a weak connection between the hands that would make it easy for the right little finger to slide off the left index finger.

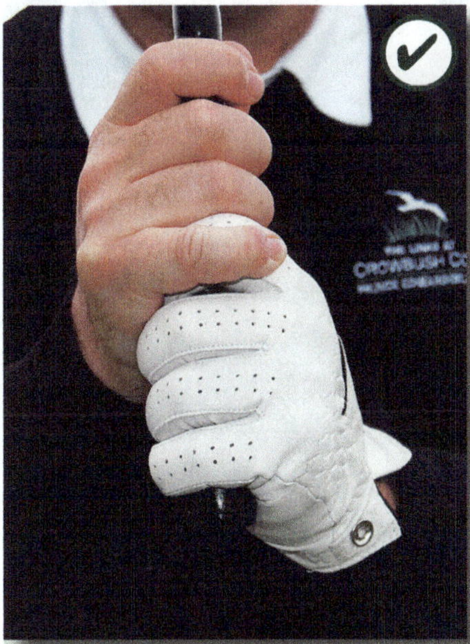

1.53

The right little finger hooks around the knuckle joint of the left index finger.

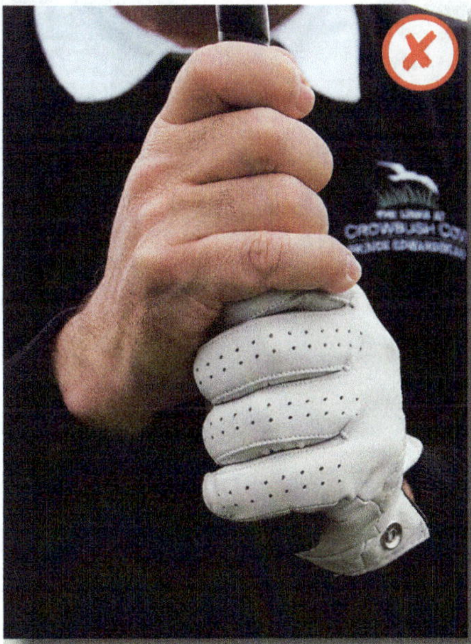

1.54

An incorrect overlapping grip. Avoid allowing the right little finger to overlap the left index finger joint for joint.

THE INTERLOCKING GRIP

In this grip, the right little finger slides between the left index finger and the left middle finger. Many golfers who have short fingers prefer this grip.

Interlock the right little finger and the left index finger

1. Slide your right little finger between your left index finger and your left middle finger, as in photograph **1.55**. The middle joint of the right little finger should contact the underside of the club shaft, more or less.
2. Photograph **1.56** shows an incorrect version of the interlocking grip. Do not slide your right little finger in too far; that is, don't allow the two palms to contact each other.

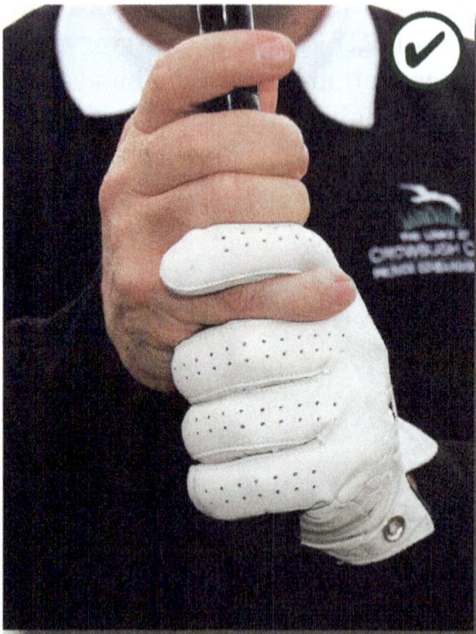

1.55

The correct amount of interlocking.

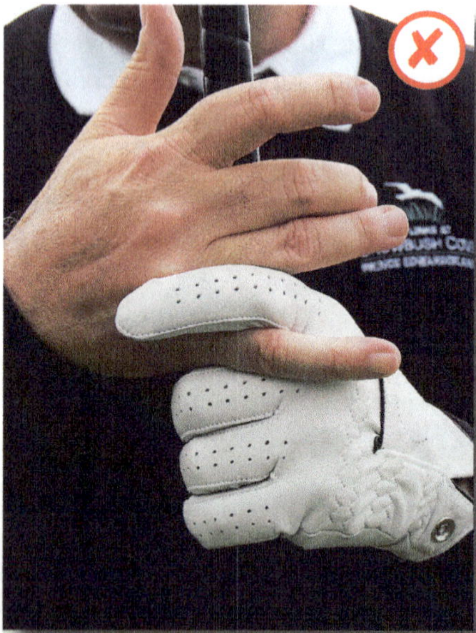

1.56

Here there is too much interlocking. The right little finger has been moved too far into the left hand.

THE BASEBALL GRIP

Although the baseball grip is the least used of the three grips, it is every bit as good as the other two, and a few superb ball strikers have used it. Keep this in mind as you decide which grip you are going to use for your swing.

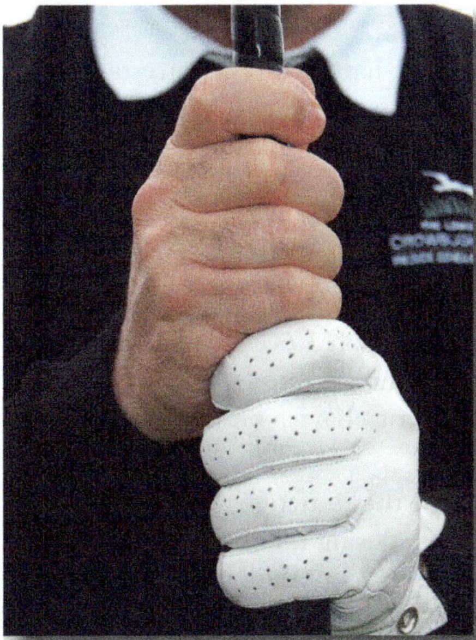

1.57

In the baseball grip, there is no overlapping or interlocking of the fingers.

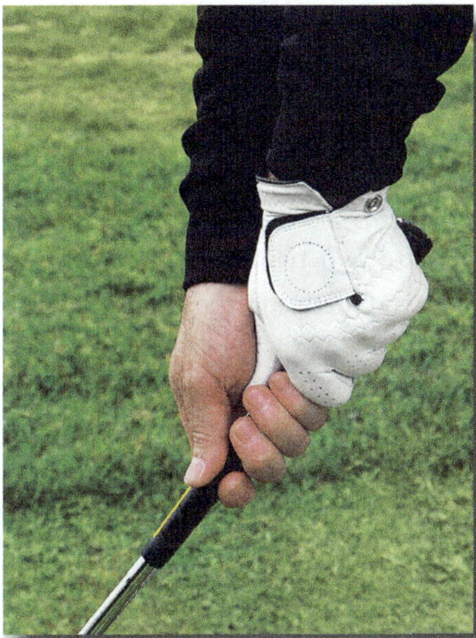

1.58

A side view of the baseball grip.

Place the right little finger snugly against the left index finger so that there is no gap between the hands (see photographs **1.57** and **1.58**), and no overlapping or interlocking of the fingers. All four fingers of each hand contact the golf club.

WHY IS THE BASEBALL GRIP NOT USED MORE OFTEN?

A few very good ball strikers – including Moe Norman, who, in my opinion, knew more about the golf swing than anyone who has ever swung a club – have used the baseball grip. So why don't more golfers use this grip?

My answer is that a youngster typically has a great deal of flexibility and a great range of motion, so the last thing he needs to do is to add more range of motion. The baseball grip adds range of motion, whereas the overlapping and interlocking grips constrain it. Therefore, a young golfer is more likely to choose the overlapping or interlocking grip than the baseball grip.

A middle-aged person is a different story. He can no longer take flexibility for granted, and his range of motion has diminished. So the baseball grip should appeal to a middle-aged golfer. If I were taking up golf today, I would seriously consider using the baseball grip.

The Right-Hand Grip

THE RIGHT HAND IS PLACED on the club after the left-hand grip has been established. Since the right palm wraps over the left thumb (see photograph **1.59**), the left hand must be in position first. The overlapping of the right hand with the left hand makes them into a single unit.

Prepare your right hand to receive the club

1. If you are using the overlapping or the interlocking grip, separate the little finger from the middle two fingers, as in photograph **1.60**. If you are using the baseball grip, keep your fingers together. In all three grips, you may separate the index finger from the middle two if you prefer to have a bit of a gap between these fingers in your final grip.
2. Keep the two middle fingers together, because they function as a unit. The two middle fingers are critical to the hand action during the golf swing. If I were to lose my little finger, index finger, and thumb, I could still use my right hand very effectively to swing a club.
3. For now, allow a gap between your right thumb and your index finger. You will close this gap later, during the final stages of the right-hand grip.

Note the angle formed by the right hand and the forearm in photograph **1.60**. This is by far the best position from which to slide your right hand under the club.

1.59

The right hand establishing initial contact with the club.

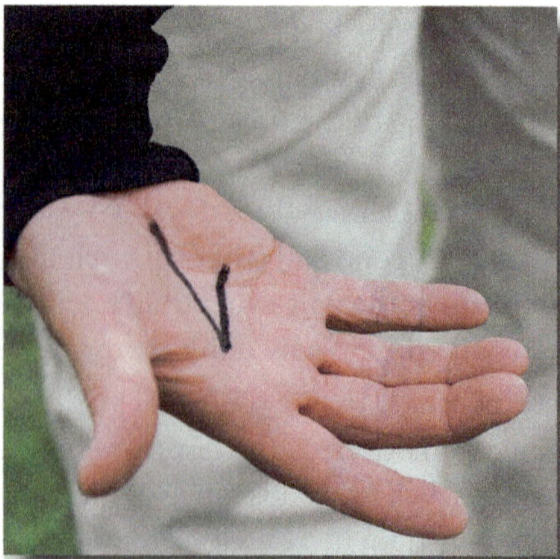

1.60

The position of my right hand as I slide it under the club.

Start your right-hand grip

1. Slide your right hand under the club. Contact seven o'clock, on the underside of the club, with the blue dots on your two middle fingers (see photograph **1.18**). Simultaneously, overlap or interlock your right little finger with your left index finger (see photograph **1.61**). If you are using the baseball grip, place the little finger snugly against the left index finger instead of overlapping or interlocking.
2. Anchor your right hand into position by contacting the underside of the club with your two middle fingers at seven o'clock. Once in this position, wrap the fingers around the club and press your right little finger down on your left index finger.
3. Now, wrap your right hand over your left thumb, as shown in photograph **1.62**. The tip of your left thumb should contact the vertex formed by the two wrinkles highlighted in black on the right palm. Photograph **1.63** is a close-up of the correct position.
4. Close the gap between your right thumb and your index finger as the right hand wraps over the left thumb. Continue wrapping your hand around the club, as in photograph **1.64**.

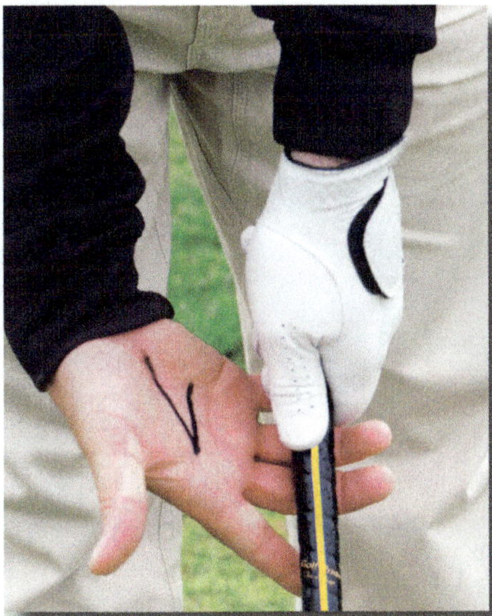

1.61

Slide the right hand under the club. Contact seven o'clock with the blue dots on the two middle fingers.

1.62

Anchor your fingers at seven o'clock and then wrap your right hand over your left thumb.

1.63

The tip of the left thumb will contact the vertex of the two wrinkles highlighted in black.

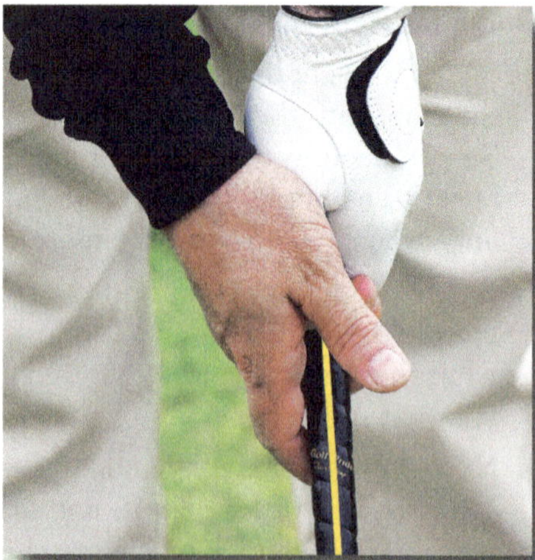

1.64

Wrap the right hand over the left thumb and close the gap between your thumb and your index finger.

1.65

Top view of the right thumb, which is positioned left of the centre of the club. The half of the thumb pad closest to the yellow stripe contacts the club; the other half does not. You can see this clearly by looking at my thumbnail.

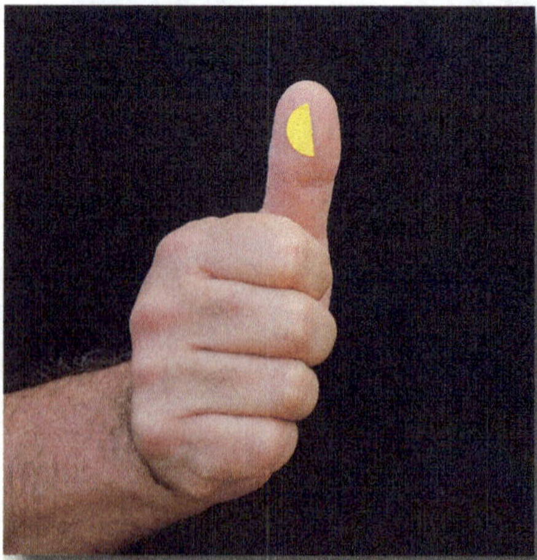

1.66

The yellow half-circle indicates the portion of the right thumb pad that makes contact with the club.

1.67

If I am in the correct position, the V of my right hand points at my chin.

5. Grip the club with your right thumb pad to the left of centre, as in photograph **1.65**. The half of the thumb pad that is closest to the palm contacts the golf club (see photograph **1.66**), while the other half does not.
6. Check to see where the V of the right hand (essentially, the line formed where the thumb and index finger meet) is pointing. It should point to your chin (see the arrow in photograph **1.67**). If the V is not pointing to your chin, start your right-hand grip again, this time sliding your right hand farther under the golf club. You might try to use 7:30 as your starting point, but you can use trial and error to determine what specific starting point you need to use in order for your hand to finish in the correct position.

This completes the step-by-step process by which to achieve a conventional golf grip. Next, I will discuss topics related to the grip.

Strong Grips and Weak Grips

YOU CAN DETERMINE whether your grip is strong or weak by observing how many knuckles of your left hand you can see once you have completed your grip. If you can see three or four knuckles, as in photograph **1.68**, you have a strong left-hand grip. The V of my right hand is pointing well to the right of my right shoulder, another sure sign that my grip is strong.

1.68

A strong grip, showing four knuckles of the left hand. The right hand is well under the club, and the V points well to the right of my right shoulder.

1.69

A weak left-hand grip shows no knuckles.

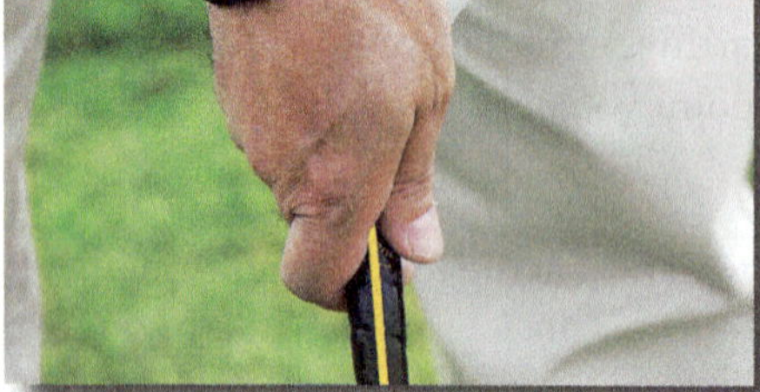

1.70

In a weak right-hand grip, the V points to the left of the left shoulder.

If you can't see any of the knuckles of your left hand, or only that of the index finger, as in photograph **1.69**, you have a weak grip. You also will have a weak grip if the *V* of the right hand points to the left of your chin or to your left shoulder, as in photograph **1.70**.

THE SIGNIFICANCE OF STRONG AND WEAK GRIPS

The forces involved in the downswing have a tendency to rotate the hands to a neutral position at the moment of impact – that is, the *V* of the right hand is pointing more or less at your chin, and the *V* of the left hand (the line formed by the left thumb and the index finger) is pointing slightly to the right of your chin

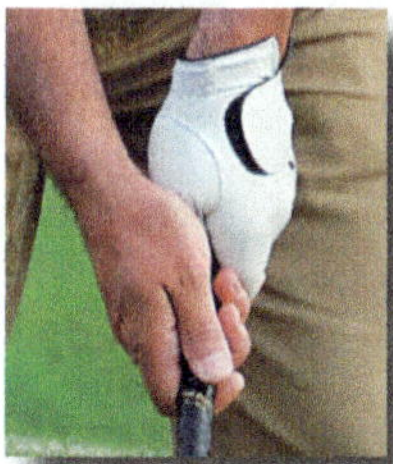

1.71

On the downswing, your hands have a tendency to adopt a neutral position at the moment of impact. A neutral position is one in which you can see two knuckles of the left hand, and the line between your right thumb and your palm points at your chin. If you start your swing with a neutral grip, and with the clubface perpendicular to the target line, you should, if all goes well, achieve a perpendicular clubface position at the moment of impact.

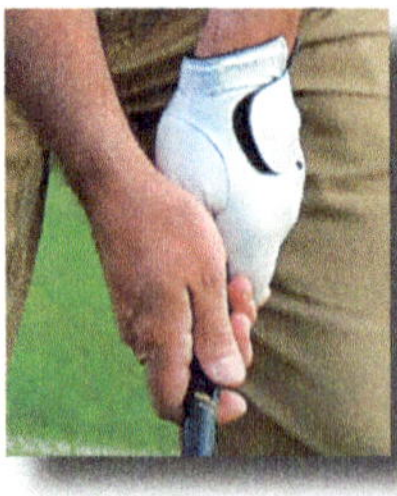

1.72

If you start your swing with a strong grip and with the clubface perpendicular to the target line, your hands have a tendency to rotate counter-clockwise to a neutral position on the downswing, and the result will be a hook, because at the moment of impact the clubface will be closed.

(photograph **1.71**). The fact that you can see only two knuckles of your left hand confirms the fact that you have achieved a neutral left-hand position.

Remember to place the clubface perpendicular to a reference line before you begin your grip. If you start your swing using a grip that is too strong, your hands will rotate back to a neutral position on the downswing. When this happens, the clubface also rotates, so that at the moment of impact the clubface will be closed, as in photograph **1.72**. This will result in a severe hook.

Starting your golf swing with a grip that is too weak produces the opposite situation. If the hands rotate to a neutral position, the clubface will be open at the moment of impact, as in photograph **1.73**. This will result in a fade or slice.

Your goal is to use a neutral grip. It can take many years for the experienced golfer to feel comfortable with such a grip. To use a neutral grip, you need the skill and

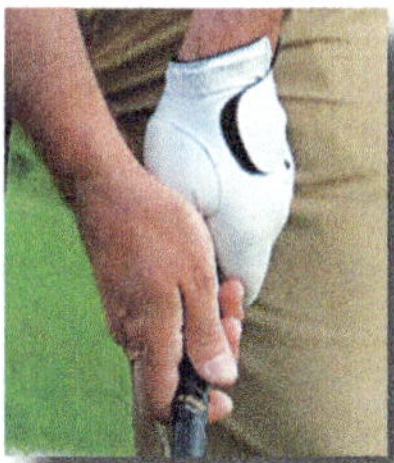

1.73

If you start your swing with a weak grip and with the clubface perpendicular to the target line, your hands have a tendency on the downswing to rotate clockwise to a neutral position, so that at the moment of impact the clubface will be open.

knowledge to return the clubface to the ball with the sweet spots aligned, skill and knowledge that the novice golfer typically lacks. He will use the strong grip, thinking that this will prevent the club from turning in his hands at the moment of impact, a false conclusion at best. The real solution would be to improve his swing and deliver the clubface to the ball with the sweet spots aligned. This takes time to learn, so using a neutral grip is really out of the question until his swing develops. A novice golfer may also gravitate toward a strong grip because it makes him feel strong, and he will be able to hit the ball hard and far. A weak grip does not give him this feeling.

A novice golfer who uses a strong grip will not be content with his shots, because a strong grip produces uncontrollable hooks. He will soon learn that his hands rotate counterclockwise on the downswing. When he realizes what has caused his hooks, he will try to control his hand action on the downswing, hoping that if he does so he will hit straight shots. Unfortunately, on the downswing the hands are not easily controlled. The novice golfer will become frustrated, and puzzled as to what to do next. The solution is to develop a grip that eliminates the tendency of the hands to rotate counterclockwise on the downswing.

The transition from a strong grip to a weaker neutral grip is likely to occur over many years, in the course of the development of your swing. Two things happen that allow you to develop and use a weaker grip. First, your swing improves, with the result that you can align the sweet spot of the clubface with that of the ball, and the impact is absorbed by the ball and the clubhead. Second, because you have too often hooked the ball, you are determined to eliminate these surprise hooks – but you now have the ability to do something about it, because your ball striking has improved considerably.

Every time you change your grip you will notice an unfamiliar feeling in your hands, but this feeling will disappear with repetition. If you progress gradually from a strong to a weak grip by making small changes, the strange feeling will be minimized, and you will become accustomed to the new feeling. The experienced golfer will continue to weaken his grip until he goes past the neutral hand position. Having gone too far, he then works back toward a stronger grip, until he finds a grip that is consistent with the hand position he wants to have at the moment of impact. This process is no different from using a fine-tuning dial on a radio: when you go too far in one direction, you turn the dial back in the opposite direction, and you continue to go in one direction and then the other until you find the correct final position.

The grip you eventually settle on will be one you know very well, because you will have spent so much time adjusting it. No one can come along and tell you exactly which grip position is best for you; only you can determine that. Most experienced, skilled golfers have spent a long time developing their grip.

Grip Pressure

ONCE YOU BECOME COMFORTABLE with both hands on the club, turn your attention to experimenting a bit with grip pressure – how tightly you hold onto the club using your fingers, thumbs, and left palm. You should do so with authority, but without inhibiting the natural freedom of your wrists. I find that I need this freedom in order to hit the shot I want to hit. I can grasp the club quite tightly with the last three fingers of each hand without losing the natural movement of the wrists, but if I apply a similar force using the index fingers and thumbs, the wrists lock up immediately. For some anatomical reason, a tight grip with the index finger and thumb impedes the natural freedom of the wrists.

Test your grip pressure

1. Hold a club parallel to the ground at hip height, using both hands.
2. Increase the pressure applied by the last three fingers of each hand and move the club up and down to test the freedom in your wrists. You should be able to apply quite a lot of pressure before you notice any loss of freedom (see photographs **1.74**, **1.75**, and **1.76**).

1.74

1.75

1.76

1.74

The starting position for testing your grip pressure.

1.75

Move the club upward.

1.76

Stop moving the club upward when you have reached this position.

3. Next, increase the pressure applied by the index finger and thumb of each hand, and move the club up and down, as before. This time you should notice a significant loss of freedom in the wrists. Grip pressure is an individual thing. Only you can discern how much pressure you are applying to the club.

GRIP PRESSURE BEFORE AND DURING THE SWING

It is important to remember to vary your grip pressure during your swing. The different stages of the swing demand different grip pressures, which we will call pressure 1 and pressure 2. When you address the ball, and during your backswing, apply pressure 1. Some instructors suggest that pressure 1 should be very light – as though you were holding a small bird. Personally, I could never follow this instruction. I always hold the club with authority, and use a fair bit of finger pressure. I neither white-knuckle the club nor restrict my wrist movement, but you would have a hard time prying my fingers off the club. But you should try the "holding a bird" approach to see if it feels comfortable for you.

On the downswing, when there is a great deal of interaction between your arms and your legs, your grip pressure should increase to pressure 2. My own experience is that it will do so automatically, in order to deal with those interactions. I feel a direct link between the pressure my hands apply to the club and my footwork and leg action. You should be able to detect this cause-and-effect relationship, because it does exist during the power phase of the golf swing.

In your follow-through, your grip pressure returns to pressure 1.

Should You Wear a Golf Glove?

THERE ARE BENEFITS to wearing a golf glove on your left hand (assuming you are right-handed). The leather of the glove is compressed when you grip the club, and forms a bond between your hand and the club. There is, however, a slight loss of sensation in your hand when you wear a glove. This is of no consequence when you are hitting full shots, but when you are chipping and putting you should remove the glove, in order to maximize the sensation in your left hand.

High-quality golf gloves are made from cabretta, which is a very thin leather that tears very easily. If there are any faults in your grip, a hole will appear in your glove in no time. This will not be the result of a manufacturing defect. The most common cause of glove tear is a movement of the club in the golfer's hand, which causes chafing between the glove and the club. The thin leather is not strong enough to withstand the chafing, so it tears.

Low-quality golf gloves, on the other hand, are made of thick leather, so they reduce the sensation in your hands too much, and I don't recommend that you wear them. If your hands don't sweat, you don't need to wear a glove. However, if you try a high-quality glove and find that you like it, continue to wear it.

Golf gloves come in various sizes, and they are marked according to the size of the palm. A glove marked "medium-large" is meant for someone with a medium-large palm and fingers of average length. One marked "medium-large cadet" is meant for someone with a medium-large palm and shorter fingers. Make sure that each of your fingers reaches the end of the glove. If you find that there is extra room, look for a cadet glove. The perfect golf glove has thin leather, fits your palm snugly, and has no extra room at the ends of the fingers.

The Modified Left-Hand Grip

WHEN I STARTED GOLFING, I used the traditional left-hand grip – holding the club in the palm of my left hand along the line between the yellow and blue dots (see photographs **1.00** and **1.03**). Later I switched to positioning the club over the blue dot and the three green dots, as in photograph **1.77**.

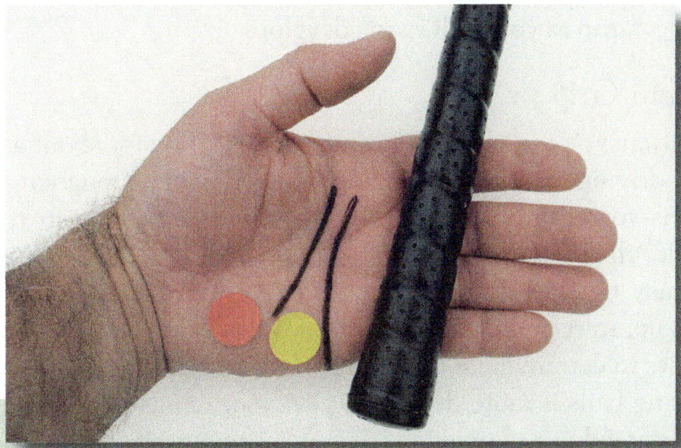

1.77

The left-hand finger grip, in which the club is placed across the green and blue dots.

When you use the green dots instead of the yellow dot, the club is lower in the palm, more in the fingers. The flesh of the green-dot area now presses against the club instead of squeezing against it.

I find that this modified left-hand grip, or left-hand finger grip, is much more comfortable than the traditional left-hand grip. You take this grip in the same way as you take the traditional left-hand grip. The only difference is that the green-dot flesh is no longer squeezed against the club. It is the last three fingers that provide the upward force on the club to counteract the downward force of the red-dot flesh.

Notice that you need strong fingers to use this grip. I found that my fingers were strong enough to withstand the force of the impact of the club on the ball without having the club turn in my hands. It helps if you know how to keep the sweet spot of the ball aligned with the sweet spot of the clubface during the swing. Chapter 3 explains how to align the sweet spots and keep them aligned during the swing – a significant benefit of knowing how to use your hands.

This left-hand finger grip allows me to generate high clubhead speed, and it is great for shaping my shots. You might think that this grip would encourage the left wrist to break down before the moment of impact. This is a common fault of the beginning golfer, and it causes all kinds of wayward shots. You will learn that correct hand action during the swing will prevent your wrists from breaking down, and will thus allow you the freedom to use a grip of this kind.

I use the traditional left-hand grip for hitting fades and for taking spin off my shots, and the left-hand finger grip to maximize spin and distance. I am used to the feel of both grips, so I don't hesitate to switch between them during a round of golf. I encourage you to start your golfing using the palm grip, and then move toward the finger grip as your golf swing develops.

Practising Your Grip

PRACTISE THE GRIP FOR ten to fifteen minutes twice a day for about a week before you visit the driving range to hit some balls. This will toughen the skin on your hands. As you practise, watch out for blisters, especially in the green-dot area. If they develop you may have to abandon your practice sessions until they heal, which may take a few days. If, after two or three days of practising, the skin toughens up, start practising three times a day. With more practice, you will develop calluses in certain areas of your hands. Once this occurs, you are ready to hit balls. Hitting balls is more demanding on your hands than simply practising the grip, so be careful not to overdo it. If you limit yourself to a half-hour practice session on the driving range you should be able to avoid blisters. Give your hands time to toughen up and form calluses before engaging in long practice sessions on the practice tee.

PRACTISE ANYWHERE

You don't need much room to practise the grip, so practise anywhere – at the office, or while watching television at home. If you have a desk job, you can use a piece of wooden dowelling about ten inches long and three quarters of an inch in diameter and practise at your desk for a few minutes at a time.

MONITOR YOUR GRIP CONTINUOUSLY

One of the interesting things about the grip is that it can change without your realizing it is doing so. In the days when I was still developing my swing, I occasionally discovered that this was happening to me. It was usually during a round of golf, when I was concentrating more on my score than my swing. Once, when I was in some tall rough and needed to muscle the ball out, I discovered that my grip was stronger than I wanted it to be. I think that's when I changed to the modified left-hand grip – without realizing I had done so. Sometime later I simply fell back to using my old grip.

Mastering the Golf Swing

IT IS AMAZING HOW OFTEN you find yourself revisiting an issue while developing an aspect of your swing. You may find this frustrating, but you will find that each time you revisit an issue the solution will be easier to implement. When you implement the same solution over and over again you will eventually become an expert in it, and it will become a permanent change. This is natural, and it's a common experience. Even after you have perfected your swing, the same old faults will resurface if you take a long layoff. But these faults become so familiar to you that you will know how to correct them. With experience, you can have your golf swing back in good shape in no time.

Simulating the Position of the Forearm, Wrist, and Hand at the Top of the Swing

NOW THAT YOU KNOW how to grip a club, we can do a little exercise. By showing you how the wrists cock and uncock during the golf swing, and simulating the correct position that the forearms, wrists, and hands achieve at the top of the swing, this exercise will provide some valuable insights.

Pick up your piece of dowelling and apply your golf grip to it. (In photographs **1.78** to **1.87** I'm using part of an old club that was cut off just below the grip.) Place your elbows on the table or desk in front of you. Notice that in photographs **1.78** and **1.79** my wrists are straight, or uncocked.

Begin with your dowel pointing straight up, as in photographs **1.78** and **1.79**, and then move your hands so that it points toward you. As it moves toward a horizontal position, the angle between your wrists and your forearms decreases, as in photographs **1.80** and **1.81**. You may notice that in photographs **1.81**, **1.83**, **1.84**, and **1.85** my shortened club is to the left of my face, and think to yourself that it should be to the right. You are correct in your thinking. These photographs were shot using the angle that would best illustrate the important points of this exercise. When I actually swing the club, my hands are positioned over my right shoulder and to the right of my face when I finish the backswing.

This exercise involves moving the dowel back and forth through ninety degrees in a vertical plane. Now that you have the idea, move it back slowly from the horizontal to the vertical position. Note that, because of the configuration of

1.78

1.79

1.80

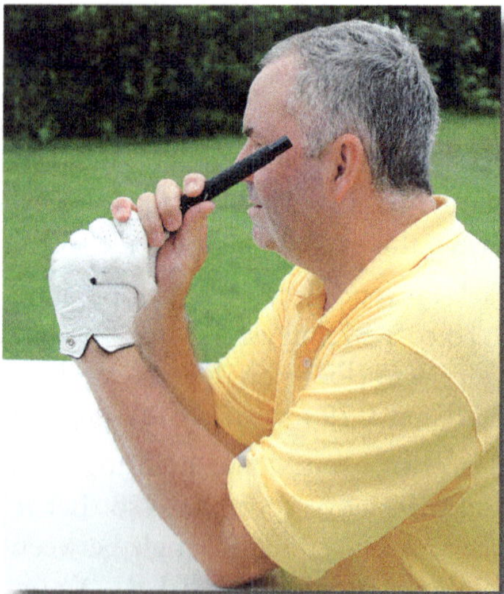
1.81

1.78 - *Apply your grip to a piece of dowelling and place your elbows on the table.*

1.79 - *My wrists are uncocked in this position.*

1.80 - *I move my club toward me by cocking my wrists.*

1.81 - *When my wrists are partially cocked, the angle between my hands and my forearms is reduced.*

1.82

1.83

1.82 - *When my wrists are fully cocked, my club is horizontal.*

1.83 - *During the backswing the wrists cock as you turn your shoulders, until at the top of the backswing the wrists are fully cocked. In this photograph I am simulating the position of the hands at the top of the backswing.*

the golf grip, your forearms rotate in response to the movement of your wrists. Note also that the dowel moves in a vertical plane (up and down) between your forearms – it does not move from side to side. When it is horizontal, as in photographs **1.82** and **1.83**, look at the angle formed by the back of the left hand and the forearm – it should be a straight line, as in photograph **1.82**.

Notice that the forearm and the edge of the left hand, as they appear on the left side of photographs **1.84** and **1.85**, form a straight line, while in the same photographs there is an angle between the back of the left hand and the forearm. This angle occurs because the left forearm rotates as the wrists cock. This is the position of the forearms, wrists, and hands that you want to achieve at the top of the backswing.

In this position, the left wrist should feel comfortable, without any undue strain or stress. If it does not, your hands will not be in the correct position at the top of the swing.

Of course, this little exercise is not the full story about how to achieve a good backswing, but it's a useful preview of some of the things that happen during it.

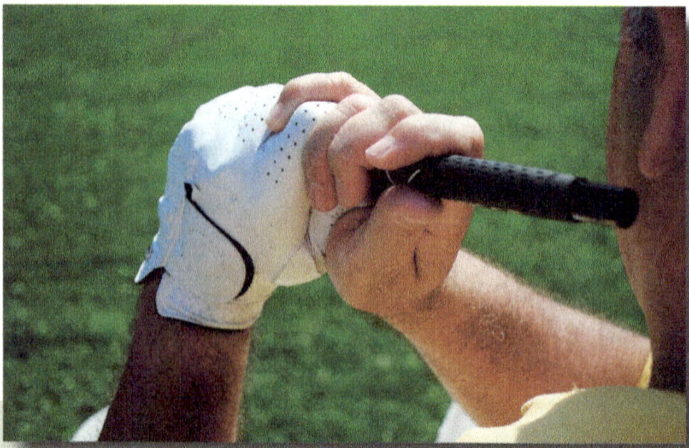

1.84

The position of the left wrist was achieved because the left forearm rotated when the wrists were cocked.

In order to move the dowel from the vertical to the horizontal you must cock your wrists. On the backswing, you do this as you turn your shoulders ninety degrees, and your forearms rotate exactly as they do during the above exercise. The movement of the dowel from the horizontal back to the vertical simulates the uncocking of the wrists. During the swing, the wrists uncock on the downswing as the shoulders unwind. In response to this uncocking, the forearms rotate in the opposite direction to the way they did on the backswing. As you will see in more detail in Chapter 3, the vertical movement of the dowel corresponds to the cocking of the hands parallel to the target line.

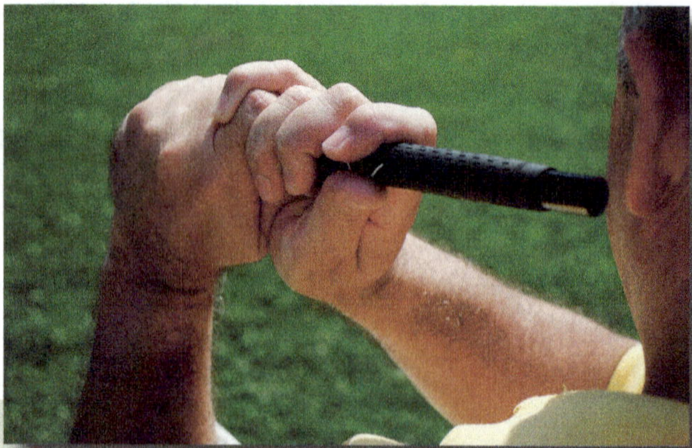

1.85

The left wrist position without a glove. Notice that the thumbs are under the club, as they are at the top of the backswing.

1.86

Stand up, straighten your left arm, partially turn your shoulders, and cock your wrists.

1.87

At the top of the swing, the shoulders have turned ninety degrees and the wrists are fully cocked.

Now, with the dowel in the horizontal position, stand up from the table, straighten your left arm, and turn your shoulders several degrees, as in photograph **1.86**.

Normally your wrists are not cocked when you begin your backswing. Therefore, during the backswing you need to turn your shoulders and cock your wrists so that the club moves in a vertical plane between your forearms, just as it did when your elbows were on the table. Continue to turn your shoulders through ninety degrees and cock your wrists until your hands are at the top of the swing, as in photograph **1.87**.

This exercise is a very simple way of experiencing the position you want to achieve at the top of the backswing. It is one thing to read instructions on how to play golf, but it is another to experience the instructions first-hand. Experiencing it first-hand helps you to believe in it. I hope this has been your experience here.

2 | Addressing the Ball

THE PHRASE "ADDRESSING THE BALL" refers to the process of taking your stance so that your body and the clubface are properly aligned in relation to your target and the ball. The accuracy of your golf shot, and its other characteristics, are determined by your stance, your body alignment, and the clubface alignment, all of which are established "at address." It is critical that you understand how to aim at your target, and learn what factors at address contribute to a successful shot. What distinguishes professional golfers is their ability to address the ball in such a way that when they swing the club they hit the shot they intend to hit.

Your address to the ball is your opportunity to fine-tune your body posture so that it gives you the best chance for a fault-free swing. This chapter describes the typical approach to addressing the ball. Once you have become familiar with it, you can introduce your own idiosyncrasies. This is normal, and if it improves your golf swing, go ahead and do it. But first learn the typical approach, and then add your personal preferences slowly, as you learn what works for you.

The Target Line

THE TARGET LINE IS THE imaginary straight line between your ball and your target that you create in your mind before every shot (photograph **2.00**). Establishing the target line should be part of your pre-shot routine. You use the target line as a

2.00

The white line depicts an imaginary target line.

reference when you align your body in relation to your intended target. You can place a representation of the target line within a few feet of your ball, to help you when you are taking aim at the distant target.

What is your target? Most of the time it will not be the flag stick. It will usually be the spot on the fairway or green where you want your ball to land so that you'll be in an advantageous position when you make your next shot. For example, if you are aiming for a fairway, you might try to land your ball on a downhill slope, in order to gain extra distance. Or you might want to land it on a spot that will enable you to make your next shot from a level lie. If you are hitting to a green, you may want to land your ball below the hole, so that you will have an uphill putt. The only time the hole itself becomes your target is when you have a realistic chance of holing your shot – that is, when you are making short putts and short chip shots.

Establish the target line

1. Stand behind your ball, directly facing your target. Stand far enough behind the ball so that you can see both your target in the distance and your ball in the foreground, as in photograph **2.01**.

2.01

Stand so that you, the ball, and your target are all on your target line.

2. Keeping the ball and the target in your sight, imagine a straight line connecting the ball to the target. Alternate your focus between the ball and the distant target by moving your head up and down in a vertical plane until you have established the line in your mind.

CHOOSE A REFERENCE OBJECT

Look for – or place on the ground – an object on the target line two or three feet in front of your ball. This reference object can be a piece of discoloured grass, a leaf, a pebble, a broken tee – anything that's big enough that you can easily see it again when you move from behind the ball to beside it. In photograph **2.02**, for instance, I have used a golf tee.

2.02

My reference object is a golf tee, which I have placed two to three feet in front of the ball.

Establish the target line from the side

1. Move from behind the ball to beside it, where you will be standing when you take your swing.
2. Find your reference object. Establish a straight line between it and your ball.
3. The line from your reference object to your ball coincides with your original target line. Since the reference object acts as a substitute for the distant target, you can ignore the distant target at this point. You can be much more accurate if you align yourself to objects close to you than if you try to align yourself to something several hundred yards away. Besides, it's easier.

Place the clubhead behind the ball

1. Stand beside the ball and hold the club in your right hand, where you normally grip it, as in photograph **2.03**.
2. Rest your right upper arm against your upper body, as in photograph **2.04**.
3. Step toward the ball with your right leg so that eighty percent of your weight is on your right foot, which should be placed perpendicular to the target line. When you are near enough to the ball, place the clubhead behind the ball with the clubface perpendicular to the target line. See photographs **2.03** and **2.04**.

2.03

Stand to the side of the ball and the target line and place the clubhead behind the ball.

If you were to extend the line made by the inside edge of your right shoe, it should cross the target line about a shoe's width to the right of the ball. In photographs **2.05** and **2.06**, notice the distance between my right foot and the club on the ground that is perpendicular to the two parallel clubs.

2.04

My right upper arm rests against my torso as I step toward the target line and place the clubhead behind the ball.

Your left foot is farther away from the target line than your right foot. Your left foot should be slightly open (pointing slightly to your left), as in photograph **2.05**. Only about twenty percent of your weight should be on your left foot – just enough to balance yourself comfortably.

Photograph **2.06** shows that with your right foot and leg closer to the target line than your left foot and leg, your shoulders and hips will be open relative to the target line. That is, your torso will point in the direction of your reference object. From this position you can easily see both your reference object and your ball. With both objects in view, you can accurately place the clubface perpendicular to the target line.

2.05

The left foot is slightly open, and farther away from the target line than the right foot.

4. As you look at the reference object and the ball, imagine a straight line between them. Place the clubhead behind the ball so that the ball is approximately opposite the clubface's sweet spot. Turn your attention to the position of the clubface. Is it perpendicular to the line between the ball and the reference object? To determine whether it is, look at the clubface and the ball, and then – without moving your head – move your eyes to the reference object. Evaluate what you have seen: is the clubface perpendicular to the line joining the ball and the reference object? If not, adjust the clubface so that it is. If you aren't sure, take another look. Look at the clubface and ball again, then move your eyes left and look at your reference object. Adjust the clubface as needed. Continue this process until you're sure the clubface is perpendicular to the line joining the ball and the reference object, as in photograph **2.07**.
5. Keeping the clubface perpendicular to the line joining the ball and the reference object, visually align the sweet spot of the clubface to the sweet spot

2.06

The hips and the shoulders are open, because the left foot is farther from the target line than the right foot.

of the ball. Do this by edging closer to or farther away from the target line with your right foot. As you do so, you will also move your torso closer to or farther away from the target line. If your right upper arm is resting against your torso, its movements will correspond with the movements of the right foot. This is why you hold the club in the right hand when you are placing the clubhead and positioning the clubface behind the ball. See photograph **2.08**.

2.07

The clubface is perpendicular to a line joining the ball and the tee; therefore, it is perpendicular to the target line.

2.08

Moving closer to the target line or farther away from it adjusts the position of the sweet spot of the clubface in relation to the sweet spot of the ball.

Using your eyes, make a rough first attempt to align the sweet spot of the clubface with the sweet spot of the ball. To align them precisely you will need to waggle the clubhead, as we will see in Chapter 3. Aligning the sweet spots using your eyes is like using the coarse-tuning knob on an old-fashioned radio. It makes for a good starting point, but you'll need to do some fine-tuning as well. Waggling the club and using the sense of touch will have the same effect as using the fine-tuning knob.

6. When you are satisfied that the clubface is perpendicular to the target line, rest the full weight of the club on the ground, with the clubhead about half an inch from the ball.

   On the golf course, be careful that you don't allow the clubhead to touch the ground too close to the ball. If the ball moves while you are addressing it, you will incur a two-stroke penalty. Also, you are not allowed to touch the ground with your club in hazards such as sand traps or water hazards.

Take Your Grip

TAKE YOUR LEFT-HAND GRIP FIRST, AND THEN YOUR RIGHT-HAND GRIP

Take your left-hand grip

1. Continue to hold the club perpendicular to the line joining the ball and the reference object. Use your right hand, because you do not want the clubface to

move out of alignment relative to the ball and the target line when you take your left-hand grip. As you take your grip, keep an eye on the clubface to make sure it does not move out of position.

2. Straighten your left arm and move your left hand toward the club. While doing so, allow your shoulders to turn until they are parallel to the target line. Remember that when you stepped toward the target line with your right foot so that you could get closer to the target line in order to place the clubhead behind the ball, your hips and shoulders became open. Your hips will remain open until you take your stance, which will happen after you complete your right-hand grip. For now, do not change the position of your lower body; concentrate on placing your left hand on the club correctly.
3. Take your left-hand grip as you were instructed in Chapter 1. When you can see two knuckles of your left hand, begin your right-hand grip.

   As you take your grip, check the position of the clubface every now and then to make sure that it remains perpendicular to the target line. If the clubface moves away from the perpendicular, shift it back to its proper alignment. If you find that the clubface is not perpendicular with the target line after you have

2.09

Proper alignment. At the moment of impact my clubface is perpendicular to the target line and my hands are in the neutral position.

completed your grip, start over. At the moment of impact you want your hands to be in their natural position – with two knuckles showing. You also want the clubface to be perpendicular to the target line. The way to achieve this is to position the clubface properly before you take your grip, and then, when you take your grip, to place your hand in the correct position relative to the clubface. Photograph **2.09** shows the correct alignment, while photographs **2.10** and **2.11** show incorrect alignments.

2.10

Improper alignment. At the moment of impact, the clubface is open rather than perpendicular to the target line, even though my hands are in the neutral position.

(Detail)

2.11

Improper alignment. At the moment of impact, the clubface is closed rather than perpendicular to the target line, even though my hands are in the neutral position.

(Detail)

Take your right-hand grip

Take your right-hand grip as you were instructed in Chapter 1. Your right arm should be flexed as you do so, unlike the left arm when you take your left-hand grip. When you flex your right arm your right elbow moves close to your right hip. To confirm to a student of the swing that he has achieved the correct arm flex, a teaching professional might slide a club in front of the student's right elbow and under his left elbow. If this club is parallel to the target line, the student's shoulders will also be parallel to the target line. Take a close look at photograph **2.12**. My right arm is flexed so that my left forearm is visible behind it, and my shoulders are parallel to the target line, and I therefore know that my right arm is flexed sufficiently that it will not hamper my address position or my swing. If your left elbow is closer to the target line than your right elbow you should be in a good position.

Now look at photograph **2.13**. Here, my right elbow is closer to the target line than my left elbow, either because my shoulders are open or because I have a weak right-hand grip. When I am in this position, a club placed over my right elbow and under my left elbow will not be parallel to the target line. If you start your backswing from this position you will do so from outside the target line, and, consequently, when you are at the top of your backswing your club will point to the left of your intended target. At the moment of impact you will likely cut

2.12

This is good arm position. My left forearm is visible from this angle because my right arm is flexed sufficiently that my right elbow is farther from the target line than my left elbow. My shoulders are parallel to the target line because my right arm is in a good flexed position. No adjustments are required.

2.13

Poor arm position. My right elbow is closer to the target line than my left elbow, and my shoulders are open as a result. To correct this – to bring my shoulders parallel to the target line – I must flex my right arm so that my left elbow is closer to the target line than my right elbow.

across the target line from outside to inside (that is, from the area in front of you that is beyond the ball to the area that is between you and the ball). As a result, you will hit either a dead straight left shot or a severe slice, depending on the position of the clubface at the moment of impact.

With both hands gripping the club correctly, turn your attention to positioning yourself in relation to the ball and taking your stance.

Relative to the Ball

POSITION YOURSELF IN RELATION TO THE BALL

AS A MATTER OF PERSONAL preference, when I position myself in relation to the ball, it is my upper body that I refer to rather than my feet or my stance. The first thing I do after completing my grip is position myself so that the ball is directly ahead of a point about three inches to the right of my left armpit, as in photograph **2.14**.

When I look at the ball I can see this area of my chest in my peripheral vision, so I find it very easy to use this area as a reference when I position myself. Using my upper body as my reference makes the positioning consistent, regardless of the width of my stance. It also helps to keep my shoulders parallel to the target line, which is something I'm always very conscious of. This awareness comes from years of consciously aligning myself to the target line before hitting every shot. You too should make it a permanent part of your pre-shot routine.

2.14

I position myself so that the ball is directly in front of the point that my right hand is indicating, about three inches to the right of my left armpit.

I never take a position in which the ball is to the left of my left armpit. Doing so would encourage open shoulders and a habit of slicing the golf ball – a habit I'm not interested in developing. Nor do I ever position myself so that the ball is to the right of my spine or directly in front of it, because these positions put the ball too far back in my stance, with the result that at the moment of impact the clubhead has not had enough time to descend to ground level, and the result is a topped shot.

USING YOUR LEFT FOOT AS YOUR POINT OF REFERENCE WHEN POSITIONING YOURSELF RELATIVE TO THE BALL

An alternative to using your upper body as your reference is to position yourself so that the ball is lined up with a point just inside the instep of your left foot. You should be aware, though, that with each change in the width of your stance, the position of your ball will change relative to your upper body.

You should make it a goal to establish a consistent impact position for yourself and hone your motor skills within the impact area. To develop these skills you want the ball in the same position for each shot. But using the instep of the left foot as a reference does not encourage this. It also does not encourage the development of a consistent impact position, and it therefore makes it more difficult to hone your motor skills within the impact area. If you use your upper body as your reference, the ball will be at the same spot in relation to your body each time, because the determination of the position of the ball relative to your body will be independent of the width of your stance.

If you use a wide stance and use the inside of your left instep as your orientation point, the ball may be opposite a point that is too close to your left armpit, and therefore too far forward in the stance, as in photograph **2.15**. You want the ball to be at a point that will ensure that the clubhead will strike it just before you have reached the lowest point of your swing.

On the other hand, if you use a narrow stance, as in photograph **2.16**, the ball will be opposite your spine, and this is too far back in your stance. From this position you will top the ball, because the clubhead will not have had enough time to descend to ground level before contacting the ball.

For most people, the best place to contact the ball is opposite a point a few inches to the right of the left armpit. As suggested above, the ball should be struck immediately before the clubhead reaches its lowest point, which will therefore be just in front of the ball. If you check your divot, you should find that it's deeper in front of where your ball was before it was struck. This is why I have always found that relating the position of the ball to my upper body works well for me, and why I have always avoided relating it to my left foot; see photograph **2.17**.

You should keep an open mind, though, and try both ways of positioning yourself in relation to the ball – using your upper body as your reference and using

2.15

If you use a wide stance and position your left foot in relation to the ball, the ball will be too far forward. If the ball is in this position, your shoulders are likely to be open to the target line.

2.16

If your stance is too narrow, the ball will be too far back, and you will top it.

your left foot – until you are able to decide which alternative works best. Go with what works for you.

2.17

With your peripheral vision, use your upper body as a reference: place yourself so that the ball is directly in front of a point on the ground that corresponds to a point approximately three inches to the right of your left armpit.

Take Your Stance

ONCE YOUR POSITION IN RELATION to the ball is to your liking, and you've taken your grip and aligned your shoulders to the target line, begin taking your stance. Taking your stance involves positioning your left foot, positioning your right foot, establishing your stance width, and distributing your body weight between your feet and within each foot. A correct stance also involves flexing the legs and bending at the waist correctly, and standing the correct distance from the ball. The correct stance will ensure that your legs are ready to maintain your balance when you swing the club.

As you can see in photographs **2.18** and **2.19**, I begin with my right foot closer to the target line than my left foot. This is a direct result of my having positioned the clubhead behind the ball while I was holding onto the club with my right hand only. Eighty percent of my weight is on my right foot, leaving only enough weight on my left foot to balance myself while I'm in this position.

When I take my stance, I position my left foot first, then my right foot. If I were to drop a plumb bob straight down from either side of my chest, the inside of each heel would touch the corresponding plumb bob. I didn't have a plumb bob with me when I took these photographs, but a club demonstrates my point equally

2.18

The position from which I begin to take my stance. My right foot is closer to the target line than my left foot, because I had to step forward with my right foot to place the clubhead behind the ball.

2.19 - *Notice that my right foot is about one shoe width to the right of the club on the ground that is perpendicular to the target line. My left foot is too far away from the target line for me to be able to swing a club, but I will position it closer to the target line before moving my right foot into position.*

well, as in photographs **2.20** and **2.21**. The width of my stance, measured from inside my left heel to inside my right heel, is equal to the width of my torso.

2.20 - *I can use a golf club as a plumb bob to establish where to place my left heel. My left heel is placed in line with the club that is hanging from the left side of my torso.*

2.21 - *I can use a golf club as a plumb bob to establish where to place my right heel. My right heel is placed in line with the club that is hanging from the right side of my torso. I have now established the width of my stance.*

It makes sense to have the width of your stance equal to the width of your torso, because the torso constitutes the mass of your body, and to stabilize this mass you need a stance that is the same width as it is. Stance width is a matter of personal preference, though, and you'll need to experiment to find out what width you prefer. Try widening your stance slightly, noting how that affects how you turn your hips and shoulders. When the movement of your hips and shoulders becomes too restricted by the width of your stance, your stance is too wide. The point at which this happens depends a lot on your flexibility.

After experimenting with wide stances, try narrowing your stance and see how it affects your ability to maintain your balance during your swing. Focus on determining the stance width that produces the best shoulder and hip turn while maintaining ease of balance as you swing your club. I found that a wide stance inhibited my shoulder turn and hip turn on my backswing, so I narrowed it to the stance shown in photograph **2.21**; my stance is equal to the width of my upper torso.

Position your left foot

Because I rest my right arm against my body when I place the clubhead behind the ball, I have to step toward the target line with my right foot, which is therefore closer to the target line than it needs to be when I hit the ball, as in photograph **2.22**.

2.22

I position my right foot closer to the target line than my left foot so that I can rest my arm against my torso as I place the clubhead behind the ball and perpendicular to the target line.

2.23

I have moved my left foot forward and slightly to my left. The toe of my left shoe is directly below my left shoulder. I can check this by hanging a golf club from my left shoulder.

At this point, my left foot is too far from the target line. Right after I have placed the clubhead perpendicular to the target line and visually aligned the sweet spots, I change the position of my left foot.

1. Transfer all of your weight to your right leg and foot, so that you can lift your left foot off the ground.
2. Now move your left foot forward and to your left, so that the toe of your left shoe is in line with your left shoulder and your left instep is in line with the left side of your upper torso, as in photograph **2.23**.

Normally I keep all my weight on my right foot only long enough to move my left foot into position. Do not worry if your left foot is not positioned absolutely where you want it. Once you reposition your right foot in the next step you can go back to your left foot and reposition it as you see fit.

Notice that I have not placed my left foot perpendicular to the target line. I have turned it out toward my left, approximately twenty-two degrees from perpendicular to the target line.

If you turn your left foot out you will find it easier to hit through the ball without encountering any interference with the momentum of your swing at the moment of impact. A turned-out left foot also encourages you to continue your swing all the way to a good follow-through position. However, turning your left foot more than twenty-two degrees may restrict your hip and shoulder turn on the backswing, depending on your flexibility, whereas turning your left foot less than twenty-two degrees encourages a full hip and shoulder turn on the backswing, but on the downswing may impede your ability to hit through the ball and continue to a full follow-through position. Experiment with several left-foot positions to discover which position works best for your swing.

Find a left-foot position that not only allows the hips and shoulders to turn without interference on the backswing, but also allows an unrestricted swing through the ball and into the follow-through. Don't use a left-foot position that is perpendicular to the target line, because that makes it difficult to follow through to a good finishing position.

Position your right foot

Once your left foot is in position, position your right foot.

1. Transfer all of your weight to your left foot so that you can lift your right foot off the ground and place it in position.
2. In order to balance yourself as you transfer weight to your left foot, you may have to straighten your legs slightly, which will mean that your weight will move toward your left heel. As you transfer your weight to your left foot, your

upper body may move slightly away from the target line. For now, be concerned with getting the weight on your left foot and balancing yourself so you can move your right foot into position.

It takes only seconds to move the right foot into position, so you will have all of your weight on your left foot for a very short time. In fact, you should move the left foot into position, move all of your body weight to the left foot, and move your right foot into position all in one continuous motion, using a one–two beat. It takes only a couple of seconds to place your feet once you get the hang of it.

3. Move your right foot back from the target line so that it is under your right shoulder. Align your right instep with the right side of your torso. Place the right foot perpendicular to the target line. The toe of your shoe and your right shoulder should both be the same distance from the target line, as in photograph 2.24.
4. Once both your feet are roughly in place, make additional adjustments to your stance until you are comfortable. Check to make sure that your shoulders, your hips, and your feet are parallel to the target line. You should feel balanced, so that it would be hard for someone to push you from where you're standing. The term that's used in hockey is "hard to knock off the puck," and the idea is equally applicable to a golfer who has taken his stance. It should be difficult to move you from your ball.

2.24

My right toe is directly below my right shoulder. If I could extend the "plumb bob" club shaft to the ground, it would touch the toe of my right shoe.

KEEP YOUR FEET EQUIDISTANT FROM THE TARGET LINE

You cannot use the distance from the target line to the toe of each foot to measure whether your feet are equidistant from the target line, because the left foot is turned out, and therefore the left toe is farther from the target line than the right toe; see photograph **2.25**.

2.25

The turned-out left toe is farther from the target line (which is parallel to the club that is lying on the ground in front of the feet) than the right toe.

There are two ways to check whether your feet are equidistant from the target line.

Method 1

1. Reach around the back of your legs and place a "test" club on the ground against your heels.
2. Move from your stance and see whether the test club is parallel to the target line. If it is, your feet were equidistant from the target line.

This method is not convenient to use, because it's difficult to reach around to place the test club against the heels, and it's difficult to see whether the test club is parallel to the target line. The best time to use this method is when you're on the practice tee, troubleshooting your alignment. Fortunately, we have another way of checking whether the feet are equidistant from the target line. Method 2 is easy and convenient to use.

Method 2

1. Place a test club across the knees, as in photograph **2.26**.
2. Compare the position of the test club to the position of the target line. If the test club is parallel to the target line, your feet are equidistant from the target

2.26

Place a test club across your knees and note whether it is parallel to the target line.

line, a perfect position for hitting a straight shot. If it is not, then your feet are not equidistant to the target line, and you can expect to hit a curved shot.

After a little practice you will not need to place a test club across your knees. A quick glance is all you'll need in order to check whether your knees are parallel to the target line, and thus whether your feet are equidistant from the target line.

KEEP YOUR RIGHT FOOT PERPENDICULAR TO THE TARGET LINE

To understand and appreciate the importance of placing your right foot perpendicular to the target line, you have to understand what happens during the transition from backswing to downswing. At the top of the backswing, the club should be parallel both to the ground and to the target line. One of the functions of the backswing is to achieve this ideal position at the top of the swing. After you have completed your shoulder turn on the backswing, you initiate the downswing by pushing from your right foot, and thereby begin to transfer your weight from your right side to your left side. By pushing from the right foot, you apply a force to your hands, which are holding the club parallel to the target line. If the right foot is perpendicular to the target line, the force applied to your hands will be parallel to the target line. As a result, when the club starts its downswing it is pulled parallel to the target line, which is exactly how the downswing should start. When you move the club in a path that is parallel to the target line, and the clubface is perpendicular to that line, you create the best chance of applying a correct blow to the ball at the moment of impact.

If your right foot is not perpendicular to the target line, your hands will be encouraged to pull the club shaft across the target line at the moment of impact. When this occurs, the clubface will direct the ball away from your target.

To appreciate the role of a perpendicular right foot, you need to feel the interaction between your foot and your hands at the beginning of your downswing. I always feel very confident when my back is perpendicular to my target line and my weight is loaded over my right foot, which is also perpendicular to my target line. When I am in this position, I know that my hands will be moving parallel to the target line at the beginning of the downswing. Once I start my downswing correctly, I know that I'm pretty much home free.

After experiencing how the right foot performs during the transition from backswing to downswing, you will understand why Ben Hogan believed in the importance of placing your right foot perpendicular to the target line. In his book *Five Lessons: The Modern Fundamentals of Golf*, Hogan is adamant – for him, that is the only correct position for the right foot. Jack Nicklaus, however, suggests otherwise. In *Jack Nicklaus' Lesson Tee*, "Lesson 26: Driving Technique," Nicklaus suggests turning your right foot a few degrees to the right to hit extra-long drives. He says that doing so will enable you to turn your hips and shoulders farther on the backswing, which allows you to hit the ball farther. Nicklaus's technique works – I have used it myself. (Note, however, that he states that for most shots he places his right foot perpendicular to the target line.)

Whose advice should you follow, Ben Hogan's or Jack Nicklaus's? While you're a novice golfer, I recommend that you keep your right foot perpendicular to the target line. Once you know how to get yourself down the target line and have internalized the sensation of doing so, you can alter your right foot position, following Jack Nicklaus's instructions. You need a bigger hip and shoulder turn when you want to hit an extra-long shot, and you can achieve this by turning the right foot slightly to the right. Placing your right foot perpendicular to the target line should be the norm for the majority of your shots, but it is perfectly acceptable to turn your right foot out when the extra-long shot is required.

If you are struggling with your swing, using a right-foot position perpendicular to the target line will encourage the correct mechanics at the top of your swing. When you need to get back to basics, this should be at the top of your list.

Get Yourself Down the Line

WHEN I SAY "GET YOURSELF DOWN THE LINE" I am referring to your ability to move your body parallel to the target line and deliver a blow to the ball in the direction of your target. When you address the ball, you align your body parallel to the target line. On the backswing, your club should be parallel to the target line when it is at hip height. At the top of the backswing, the club should again be parallel to the target line. On the downswing, to initiate the leg action, direct a push from the right foot parallel to the target line. As your weight is transferred from the right side of the body to the left side, the hips become parallel to the target line for an instant as they slide into position. As the downswing progresses, the hips continue to unwind and cease to be parallel to the target line, but now it's the shoulders that are parallel to the target line. When the shoulders are parallel to the target line, the arms should move in the same direction as the target line. If your hand action is correct, the clubhead will travel along the target line, and the clubface will be perpendicular to the target line when it strikes the ball. Achieving all these conditions during the swing, or "getting yourself down the line," is what produces straight and accurate shots.

Hal Sutton's swing exemplifies the idea of getting yourself down the line. Hal is well known for hitting accurate shots, and much of his success can be attributed to his ability to get down the line. Watch Hal hit a few shots and you will quickly understand this term.

Distance from the Ball

YOUR ADDRESS POSITION should be the same for every club you swing, and every time you address the ball. Your arms hang from the same position each time, so the distance you stand from the ball will be determined by the length of the club you are using. Thus, when you are adjusting the distance you stand from the target line, it is not the position of your arms that you should change, but the distance between your body and the target line.

The novice golfer will vary the distance he stands from the ball by changing his arm position. He will increase his distance from the ball by moving his arms away from his upper body, and move his arms closer to his body when he needs to stand closer. But this is incorrect. If you want a consistent golf swing, your arms should hang in the same position for every shot you hit.

A significant benefit of using the same address position shot after shot is that it helps develop the motor skills that create a consistent swing. If your arms hang in the same position for every club, you are able to swing every club the same way. This allows your body to fine-tune its motor skills, especially through the impact zone, where highly refined motor skills are most needed.

The arm position

The process of determining your correct arm position is straightforward.

1. Take your grip and your address position.
2. Remove your left hand from the club but continue holding the club in your right hand.
3. With your left hand, hold the butt of a second golf club between your eyes so that it touches the bridge of your nose. Let the club hang freely from the bridge of your nose, as in photograph **2.27**.

2.27

Hang a club from the bridge of your nose and check the club's position in relation to your right hand.

2.28

Standing too far from the ball. Notice the gap between my right hand and the club hanging from the bridge of my nose.

2.29

Standing too close to the ball. Notice that my right hand extends beyond the club hanging from the bridge of my nose.

Your arms are hanging in the right position when your right index finger and thumb are directly below the bridge of your nose. In photograph **2.27**, the club that hangs freely from the bridge of my nose touches my right index finger and thumb. I therefore know that my right hand is directly below the bridge of my nose and my right arm is in the correct position. I am standing the correct distance from the ball.

In photographs **2.28** and **2.29**, the hanging club test shows that I am not standing the correct distance from the ball. You can apply this test to any club you are using. Your arms should hang the same way regardless of which club you are addressing the ball with. It is the length of the club that determines how far you stand from the ball.

EXCEPTIONS TO THE NORM

In the history of golf, there have been a few individuals who have stood farther from or closer to the ball than what conventional wisdom advocates. For those individuals, the test of acceptability becomes whether or not they can consistently hit pure shots from their abnormal arm position. If they can, they should continue to deviate from the norm.

The test for exceptions is nearly always the same: can the golfer achieve pure shots consistently using the unconventional approach? If the answer is yes, then things should be left as they are. An experienced teaching pro knows when to make changes and when to leave things alone.

Leg Flex

WHETHER YOU ARE TALL or short, your hands hang approximately the same distance from the ground as everyone else's. For this reason, golf club manufacturers produce clubs of the same length for all golfers. Minor adjustments to a standard set of clubs can custom-fit them to your precise stature, but nothing more is required. Since tall golfers and short golfers use the same clubs, tall golfers flex their legs more and bend more from the waist than short golfers. Short golfers stand straight-legged and bend at the waist only a little.

Establish your leg flex

1. Address the ball at the proper distance from the target line. Stand erect and hold the club horizontally, as in photograph **2.30**.
2. Without bending at the waist, flex your legs so that the weight of your body is centred in front of your heels, as in photograph **2.31**. Once your weight is distributed evenly on all parts of the feet, do not flex your legs any further.
3. Bend from the waist, making sure that you keep your back straight, and position the clubhead behind the ball, as in photograph **2.32**.

2.30

When you have established the correct distance from the ball, stand erect with your arms extended so that the club is more or less horizontal.

2.31

My legs are flexed, so the weight is centred in front of my heels.

2.32

My legs are flexed and my back is straight: I'm in good address position. Now I'm ready to waggle the club.

2.33

Two tests for checking your leg flex and the bend at your waist.

4. To check your leg flex, hang a golf club from your buttocks, as in photograph **2.33**. The club should hang a couple of inches behind your heels. The exact distance will vary depending on your height – for shorter golfers, the

2.34

Correct leg flex distributes the body weight in the middle area of the feet. Here, the butt end of a club indicates the front limit of this area, at the base of the toes; the rear limit is the front of the heel.

club will hang closer to the heels than for taller golfers. This makes sense, since tall players bend more from the waist and require more leg flex than shorter golfers.

To practise your leg flex and the bend from your waist at home, stand in front of a full-length mirror and imagine a vertical line extending down the middle

2.35

If your weight is too far forward, you will have the urge to step forward in order to regain your balance.

2.36

If your weight is on your heels, your legs will feel too heavy to be used effectively during your swing.

of your body (the white line in photograph **2.33**). You should see an equal amount of your body on either side of the imaginary vertical line; I like to picture a kebab with an equal amount of food on each side of the skewer. When your leg flex is correct, the body weight is distributed in the "middle" area of each foot, the area from the front of the heel to where the toes join the foot; see photograph **2.34**. If your body weight is based in that area, your legs should feel lively and ready for action. A golf swing needs lively legs.

If you position your body weight too far forward, so that it is centred at the point in your feet shown in photograph **2.35**, you will lose your balance, and will want to step forward to avoid falling over.

On the other hand, if you centre your body weight over your heels, your legs will feel extremely heavy. It is impossible to use your legs when all of your weight is over your heels, at the point indicated in photograph **2.36**. Remember that lively leg tension, which is is needed for a sound golf swing, is created by the proper distribution of weight in each foot.

Chin Up

IT IS INTERESTING TO OBSERVE the chin position of an amateur golfer when he is swinging a club. I don't know why, but the average golfer tends to lower his chin almost to his chest when hitting a ball, as in photograph **2.37**. He seems to find comfort in doing this.

2.37

If you lower your chin to your chest your shoulder turn will be blocked, so you must avoid doing so when you address the ball.

2.38

If I hold my chin up, my shoulders have room to turn. Always reserve the room under your chin for your shoulders.

When you walk, though, you keep your chin up so that you can see where you're going, and you should do the same thing when you swing your club and hit your ball. Your shoulders need room to turn under your chin (photograph **2.38**), so when you bend from the waist you must make a conscious effort to keep your chin up.

Set-up to Hit a Straight Shot

TO PREPARE FOR CHAPTER 3's lesson on the action of the hands, all you need to know is how to grip the club and how to address the ball to hit a straight shot. This is also the best address position to use if you want to correct a fault in your swing or to develop the mechanics of your swing – it will give you the purest feedback. If you want to hit a dead-straight shot, you must make sure that the position of the clubface at the moment of impact is perfect. If your shot does not fly straight toward your target, you know that there's a fault in your swing that needs attention.

If you confine yourself to hitting straight shots while you are developing your golf swing, you are less likely to develop a preference for hitting a fade or a draw. On the other hand, if you consistently set up for either a fade or draw, you may find it hard to hit the opposite shot when the occasion demands it. Most golf courses require the ability to shape shots both ways, so it's an advantage not to develop a preference for hitting one or the other. The only difference between hitting a straight shot and a curved one is the address position. There is a slight difference in the position of the legs at the moment of impact too (because of the different address set-up), but this book focuses on the hand action of the golf swing, and all you need for that is a straight-shot address position.

Jack Nicklaus can teach you how to hit curved shots in about five minutes. I do not know whether his teacher taught him this skill or whether he learned it on his own. What I do know is that his method works beautifully. To learn how Jack Nicklaus hits curved shots, read *Jack Nicklaus' Lesson Tee*. In "Lesson 16: Slicing," he describes how he sets up to the ball to hit fades. His method is simple and effective. I cannot improve on it, so I see no reason to rewrite the lesson here.

It is best to use the straight shot when you're on the practice tee working on your swing, whereas on the golf course the shot that is used to score with is the fade or the draw. A professional golfer practises hitting fades or draws so that he can consistently fade or draw the ball the same amount each time. For example, he may train himself to hit a draw that curves an average of fifteen feet. On the course, he will then aim eight feet to the right of his target. If he hits his average draw, the ball will finish seven feet to the left of the hole. If he does not hit his average draw but draws the ball seventeen feet, his ball will finish nine feet to the left of his target. Not a bad mis-hit. However, when you are trying to hit a straight shot, a small error may cause the ball to finish fifteen to seventeen feet to the left or the right of the hole – quite a difference compared to being able to anticipate the curve of your shot. Use the straight shot on the practice tee to fine-tune the mechanics of your swing, and then, when you have developed your swing, learn to hit the curved shots, and use them on the course to finish close to the hole and improve your score. This is the way of the professional golfer.

3 | The Hand Action

IS THERE A RELATIONSHIP between the movement of the hands during the golf swing and the effectiveness of the swing? My answer is yes. You won't see this relationship when you watch an amateur golfer swing a club, but if you watch a professional you will. The correct movement of the hands allows the clubface to strike the ball with a precise force, and the precision and other characteristics of the force with which the ball is struck will determine the quality of the shot and its flight pattern. If your hand action is faulty, this force will be so compromised that you will produce a bad shot. I have observed this for more than thirty years, especially among amateurs.

The way the hands move determines how the body moves to execute a correct swing. Imagine that I am an engineer who designs golf swings. The mechanics of the hand action have been specified and I am not allowed to change them – they are written in stone. On the other hand, I am given the flexibility to design body movement as I see fit. My assignment as a golf swing design engineer parallels the challenge an amateur golfer faces in developing his swing. The amateur golfer should first learn the proper hand action, and then learn how the shoulders and hips must move to accommodate the mechanics of that hand action. Proper footwork and leg action will facilitate the hip turn, which will then affect the shoulder turn. Thus, the hand action influences the the entire swing.

This chapter will teach the correct movement of the hands, and Chapter 4 will present a method of coordinating the shoulder turn with the movement of the hands. I do not teach the action of the lower body – the hips, the legs, and the feet – because existing literature deals adequately with these aspects of the golf swing.

The action of the hands is the most fundamental building block of the swing. I have observed the swings of many amateurs, and have noted that they tend to lack proper hand action. I know of only one person whose use of proper hand action seems to have been instinctive. Otherwise, the only people I see using proper hand action are the touring professionals. As I mentioned at the beginning of this book, Moe Norman observed that the amateur golfer "waves at the golf ball." I could not agree more. I see the same waving that Moe saw, and I have seen it for more than three decades.

In this book I have limited myself to teaching the hand action of the golf swing. To explain the interaction between the hands and the body would require another book. Meanwhile, I hope what I offer will point you in the right direction. Once you are on the correct path, I am confident that you will discover the other facets of correct hand action and how the body moves to accommodate it.

In the first two chapters I explained how to grip a club and how to address a ball, because you need to learn these lessons before you face the most important lesson of all: the correct action of the hands during your swing.

According to conventional wisdom, the most important lesson you need to learn in all of golf concerns the grip. I disagree. No matter how good your grip, it is simply impossible to strike the ball purely if your hand action is faulty. I have seen golfers who, although their grips were poor, used good hand action in their swing, and consequently were able to produce excellent shots. On the other hand, I have seen many, many good golf grips that did not produce good hand action. From these observations, I have concluded that the lesson that teaches the action of the hands during the swing is more important than the one that teaches the grip. The evidence speaks for itself. The lesson on the grip is necessary, but it is only a prerequisite to the lesson on the hand action.

The Waggle Isolates the Hand Action

IN A SOUND GOLF SWING, the hand action dictates the movement of the body. We can take advantage of this fact when we are learning the hand action by concentrating solely on it, and taking the body movement for granted. We can do this by standing in the address position, which involves no body movement, and waggling a club. Because this position simulates the position of the swing at the moment of impact, it is an ideal position from which to learn the mechanics of the hand action.

After you have learned the mechanics of the hand action by waggling the club, the next step is to coordinate the shoulder turn with the hand action. If you do not do so, your shoulders will interfere with your hands.

I will explain my method for coordinating shoulders with hands in Chapter 4. My method builds on the expertise of a highly respected former touring professional, Paul Runyan. The golfing masses have ignored Runyan's short-game techniques, but I have never understood why, and I find it troubling. My method allows you to isolate your shoulder turn, monitor it, and adjust it to your hand action. This may seem strange, but it works.

The most intricate and critical part of the golf swing is the coordination of the movement of the hands, the wrists, the arms, and the shoulders. When you learn the waggling of the club as I describe it below, you are learning to isolate the hand action so that you can focus on getting it right. Once you've done that, you must combine that correct hand action with the movements of your upper and lower body.

3.00

I begin at the address position.

3.01

The clubhead has begun moving away from the ball.

3.02

The clubhead is now inside the target line.

3.03

The clubhead is now parallel to the target line.

3.04

The clubhead is approaching the ball before the moment of impact.

3.05

The clubhead is now back to where it was when I started.

Look at photographs **3.00** to **3.05** and see if you can detect any logic in the way I waggle the golf club. If you can't, don't worry – this chapter will cover the logic of the waggle in detail.

You should waggle the club before each shot you hit, once you have satisfied yourself that your address position is what you want it to be. When you have finished waggling the club, you can start your takeaway and progress into your backswing.

When I want to assess a person's golf swing knowledge and skill level, the first thing I look at is the action of his hands as they waggle a club. If I see proper hand action, I will know that the person is either a very good amateur golfer, a professional golfer, or simply a person who naturally uses his hands correctly. If the hand action is different from what I know it should be, I will know that the person is an amateur golfer. According to my observations, correct hand action during the swing is a learned skill, one that is exhibited primarily by touring professionals.

The Purpose of the Waggle

THE WAGGLE SERVES TWO PURPOSES. First, the hand action of the waggle provides a way to align the sweet spot of the clubface with the sweet spot of the ball. Note that it is the sweet spot of the clubface that you align with the sweet spot of the ball, not the other way around. The clubface is moveable, but if the ball moves you incur a two-stroke penalty. Second, the hand action preserves the alignment of these sweet spots as the club pivots through ninety degrees on the backswing, and finishes parallel to the target line at the top of the backswing. The alignment of the sweet spots is preserved on the downswing as the result of correct hand action, and thus one achieves maximum compression of the ball at the moment of impact. Correct hand action provides a means of returning the clubface to a position perpendicular to the target line at the moment of impact – a requirement for hitting pure and accurate shots.

Have you ever wondered why shots by the touring pros rip through the air with a distinctive sound? This ripping sound occurs because the ball undergoes maximum compression at the moment of impact, with the result that it flies off the clubface at maximum velocity. You can only achieve maximum compression of the ball and produce the sound of the ball ripping through the air if you have the sweet spots aligned at the moment of impact. When you consider the speed at which the clubhead moves during the swing, maintaining the alignment of the sweet spots throughout the swing is no small feat, and it can only be achieved by means of correct hand action.

Another Clock Analogy

IN CHAPTER 1, WE USED THE IMAGE of a clock to help explain the correct right-hand grip. Now we can use the clock again to illustrate, in a simple, direct way, the essence of the waggle. Look at photograph **3.06,** and note that we start with the clock's hand at twelve o'clock. (I have modified the clock so that it has only one hand – that's all I need to make my point.)

In photograph **3.07**, I move the clock hand by pressing against its short extension. The point at which I apply the pressure is important, because it represents what I do when I am waggling a golf club. Later, I will relate the pressure I am applying to the clock hand to the force I apply to the club.

I stop pressing the short extension of the clock hand when it points to three o'clock, as in photograph **3.08**. For our analogy, we do not need to pivot the hand any farther.

When I move the hand back to twelve o'clock I apply the pressure to the long portion of the hand rather than the extension; see photograph **3.09**.

I stop pushing on the hand when it points to twelve o'clock again, as in photograph **3.10**.

3.06

3.07

3.08

3.09

3.10

3.06 - *The clock's hand is at twelve o'clock.*

3.07 - *I apply pressure to the short extension of the clock's hand.*

3.08 - *When the hand points to three o'clock, I stop applying pressure to it.*

3.09 - *I now apply pressure to the long portion of the hand to begin pivoting it back to twelve o'clock.*

3.10 - *The end position of our pivoting cycle. I can now stop pushing on the hand.*

So far we have observed that the clock hand pivots through ninety degrees as it goes from twelve o'clock to three o'clock, and then back to twelve o'clock. Notice that the pivot point remained fixed, or static. We should also observe that the distance between the tip of the clock hand and the static pivot point remains constant.

RELATE THE CLOCK IMAGE TO THE WAGGLE

How do these observations relate to waggling a golf club? If you imagine that a ball resting on the target line marks the twelve o'clock position on the clock, the target line will be parallel to a line connecting nine o'clock and three o'clock, as in photograph **3.11**.

Instead of the hand of a clock, we have a golf club, which includes the grip, the shaft, and the clubhead. The tip of the clock hand is represented by the clubhead and clubface. Pointing the tip of the clock hand at twelve o'clock is analogous to placing the clubface behind the ball and perpendicular to the target line, as you do when you address the ball; see photograph **3.12**. Imagine yourself aligned parallel to a line between nine o'clock and three o'clock.

The point where the left thumb pad contacts the club is analogous to the clock's pivot point. The left thumb pad is the pivot point of your golf grip, whether you're waggling the club or swinging it. See photographs **3.13** and **3.14**.

The two middle fingers of your right hand are placed under your left thumb pad when you hold the club, as in photograph **3.15**. Using the clock analogy, they are directly under the pivot point of the clock hand, and the left thumb pad is directly on top of it. The right index finger and thumb are slightly ahead of the clock's pivot point on the long side of the clock hand. Regardless of what grip you use,

3.11

The clock image applied to the golf course.

3.12

3.12 - *Placing the clubface perpendicular to the line joining the ball and the target line is just like pointing the tip of the clock hand at twelve o'clock.*

3.13 - *The pivot point of the waggle is the left thumb pad.*

3.14 - *The black arrow points to the pivot point of the clock hand.*

3.15 - *The two middle fingers of the right hand are under the left thumb pad.*

3.16 - *The short extension of the clock hand represents that part of the golf club grip where I place the last three fingers of my left hand.*

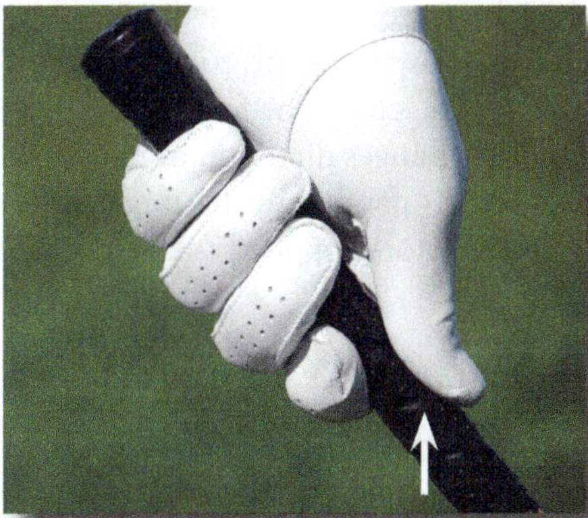

3.13

3.14

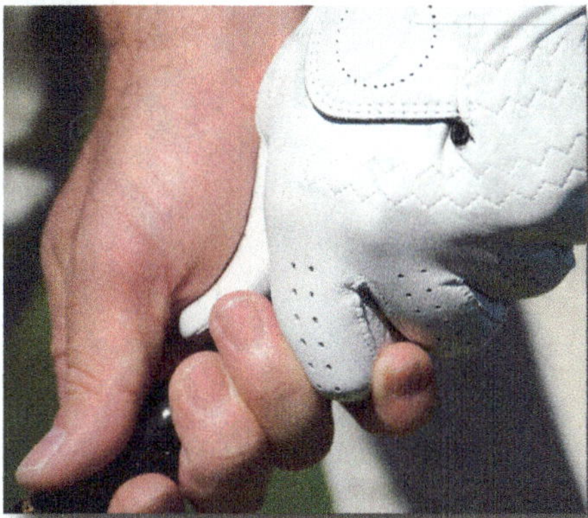

3.15

3.16

the little finger of the right hand is slightly behind the clock's pivot point on the short extension side; see photograph **3.15**.

The short extension of the clock hand corresponds to part of the club held by the last three fingers of the left hand; see photographs **3.16** and **3.17**.

You move the clock hand from twelve o'clock to three o'clock by applying pressure to the short extension. The pressure is always perpendicular to the hand itself, but it changes direction continuously as the hand pivots through ninety degrees; see photograph **3.18**. Initially, pressure is applied in the direction of nine o'clock – parallel to the target line – but as the clock hand pivots the pressure continuously changes direction. When the tip of the hand reaches three o'clock, the force is applied perpendicular to the target line.

After I have taken the address position, with the clubhead behind the ball and perpendicular to the target line, and with the pivot point – the left thumb pad – strictly controlled so that it does not change its position, I apply a force with the last three fingers of my left hand parallel to the target line in the direction of the target (see photograph **3.19**). This force causes my left hand to pivot about my left thumb pad. As my left hand pivots, so does the club. The force applied to the club is always perpendicular to the club, but it changes direction as my hand and the club pivot. The club pivots until the shaft is parallel to the target line, as in photographs **3.20** and **3.22**. At this point, the force applied to the club is perpendicular to the target line.

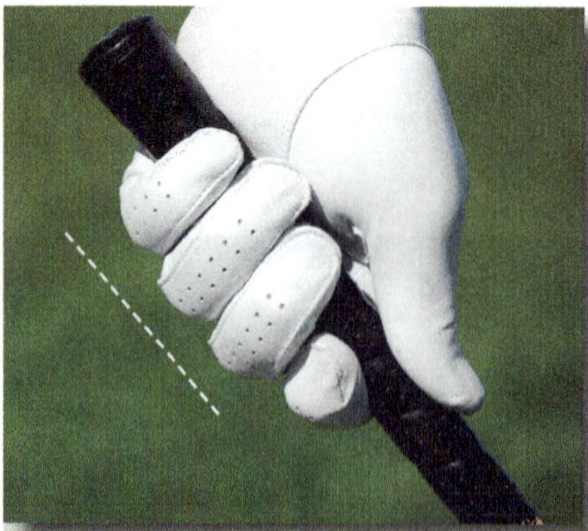

3.17

The white line represents the short extension of the clock hand, which corresponds to the last three fingers of the left hand.

3.18

The direction of the force applied to the short extension of the clock hand changes continuously, as indicated by the arrow.

3.19

The last three fingers apply the initial force to the club in the direction of the target and parallel to the target line. The arrow represents this force.

3.20

The force applied to the club by the last three fingers of the left hand finishes in a direction perpendicular to the target line.

To pivot the clock hand back to twelve o'clock, as in photograph **3.21**, I now apply a deliberate force to the long segment of the hand.

3.21

Apply pressure to the long portion of the clock hand.

3.22

As the club pivots from the ball to a position parallel to the target line, the last three fingers of the left hand exert a force against the club grip perpendicular to the target line. This force is represented by the yellow arrow. To pivot the club back to the ball, the right hand exerts pressure against the club grip perpendicular to the target line. This force is represented by the white arrow.

3.23

Use your right hand to apply a force against the club to pivot it back to the ball.

Pivoting the clock hand from three o'clock to twelve o'clock is analogous to pivoting the club from a position parallel to the target line (photographs **3.21** and **3.22**) back to the address position, where it is perpendicular to the target line. Instead of the last three fingers of the left hand applying the force against the club, it is now the right hand that applies the force (see photographs **3.22** and **3.23**).

The club still pivots about the left thumb pad. The force originates from the right hand, but both hands use the left thumb pad to pivot the club back to the ball. Initially, the force applied to the club by the right hand is perpendicular to the target line. The force is applied only long enough to overcome the inertia required to redirect the club. Once the club is pivoting, the right hand needs to apply only minimal force – a force sufficient to continue pivoting the club but nothing more. The left hand need only apply sufficient force to guide the clubhead back to the ball.

Pivot Your Hands Around a Piece of Masking Tape

THE PURPOSE OF THIS EXERCISE is to learn how it feels to rotate your left forearm as it moves to the left and away from your body – or, more generally, how it feels to pivot your left hand about a stationary pivot point. If you use a table and a piece of masking tape, and follow the instructions, you will be forced to move your left hand and forearm in the very specific manner that's required for correct hand action. The goal is to learn the sensation associated with this movement. This will be your way of monitoring your hand action during your swing.

I prefer to start the lesson using the controlled environment of a table, because it is very easy to pivot your left hand incorrectly when you use a golf club, and I want to minimize the possibility of introducing unnecessary errors. Pivoting a club correctly is easy once you learn what to do and what to avoid. To waggle a club correctly, it is critical that you know how to pivot the left hand about a stationary pivot point.

Prepare the set-up

1. Find a table or desk of standard height; a kitchen table or a computer table will do.
2. Stick a piece of masking tape half an inch wide and an inch and a half long on the lower left corner of your table, as in photograph **3.24**.
3. Place your left thumb pad on the masking tape and straighten your left arm, as in photograph **3.25**.

4. Position your upper body opposite the tape so that the tape is three inches to the right of the line of your left armpit, in line with the position of the golf ball when you take your address position.
5. Take your stance and align yourself parallel to the side of the table you are facing, as you do when you align yourself parallel to the target line when you prepare to hit a straight shot; see photograph **3.26**.
6. Establish a good address position for the rest of your body, as you would if you were preparing to hit a real golf shot.
7. The right hand is not used in this exercise, so let your right arm hang naturally at your side.

3.24

Stick a piece of masking tape on the table.

3.25

Straighten your left arm and place your left thumb pad over the masking tape.

3.26

Align your stance so that your hips and shoulders are parallel to the side of the table you are facing.

Pivot your left hand

1. With your left thumb on the masking tape, as in photograph **3.27**, push the last three fingers of your left hand to the left. As you do this, your hand will rotate in an arc, the centre of which is your left thumb pad (see photograph **3.28**). Allow the left thumb pad to rotate over the masking tape as your left hand pivots along the leftward arc; see photograph **3.29**.

   The last three fingers and the short extension of the clock hand move in exactly the same way. As the clock hand pivots from twelve o'clock to three o'clock, the short extension moves leftward along an arc between six o'clock

3.27

The initial position of the left thumb pad.

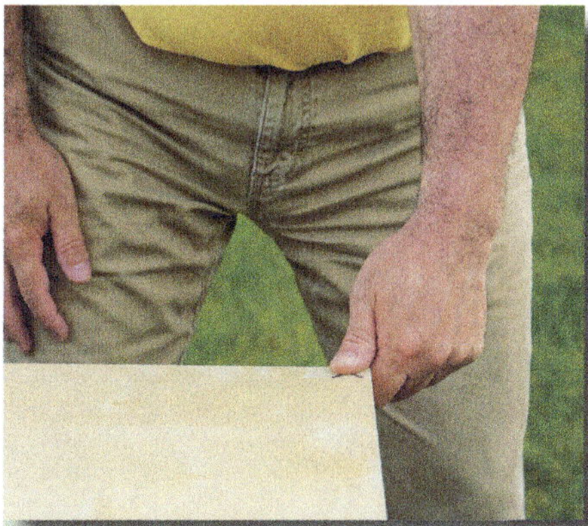

3.28

When you push your last three fingers to the left, your left hand will rotate along an arc whose centre is the left thumb pad.

3.29

The left thumb pad rotates on the masking tape while the left hand rotates.

and nine o'clock. Similarly, as your left hand pivots from its starting position to a position parallel to the side of the table you are facing, it moves leftward along an arc. The last three fingers move along an arc equal in radius to the distance from the left thumb pad to the last three fingers.

In the following sequence of photographs, it may appear that my left elbow is bent. In fact, it is not. The purpose of this exercise is to learn how to move your left hand and your forearm simultaneously about a static pivot point. Keep your elbow straight, to make sure you are concentrating on your hand and your wrist and coordinating their movements correctly.

2. In order to accommodate the movement of the pivoting left hand, the forearm moves slightly. From its original position (photographs **3.30** and **3.31**), it moves to the left and away from your body (photographs **3.32** and **3.33**).

3.30

A front view of the initial forearm position.

3.31

A side view of the initial forearm position.

3. As your hand pivots and your forearm rotates, keep your left arm straight – don't bend your elbow.
4. Continue to pivot your left hand about the masking tape until you can detect by feel and sight when the back of the left hand is parallel to the side of the table facing you, as in photographs **3.34** and **3.35**.

   To learn when to stop pivoting your left hand, watch as it approaches a position parallel to the side of the table facing you. Concentrate on the feeling you have in your hand, wrist, and forearm. When your hand is parallel to the side of the table facing you, you should have a distinct feeling in your left forearm, wrist, and hand that tells you not to pivot any farther. It requires a little trial and error to discern and learn this sensation. Try pivoting your hand beyond the parallel position and note the feeling in your forearm, wrist, and hand. If

3.32

My left forearm has rotated and moved to my left to accommodate the pivoting left hand.

3.33

My left forearm moved away from my body as my left hand pivoted through ninety degrees.

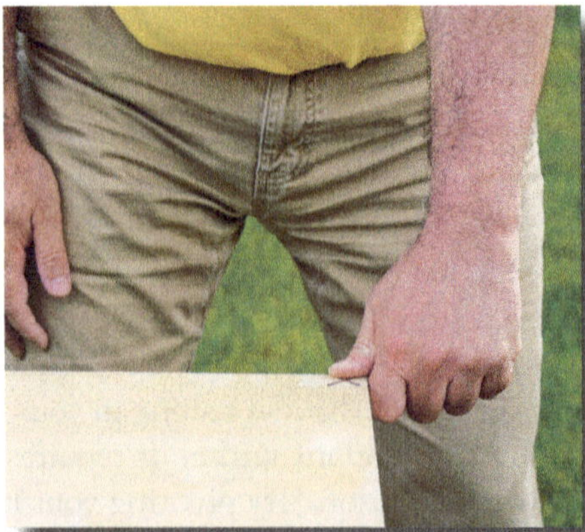

3.34

The back of my left hand is now parallel to the side of the table facing me.

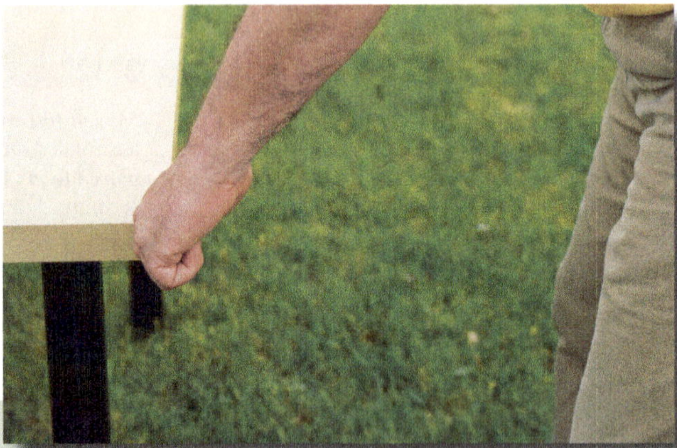

3.35

The back of my left hand is parallel to the side of the table facing me.

you pivot the hand more than ninety degrees you should feel a tension in your forearm, wrist, and hand; use this tension as a signal that you have pivoted your hand too far. The table exercise forces you to pivot your left hand, wrist, and forearm correctly. It also teaches you the sense memory that is associated with correctly pivoting the left hand. Sensation is the essential language of communication during the golf swing.

On the golf course, away from the practice tee, you will have to use your sense memory to monitor your hand action while you waggle or swing a club. This is the best and most immediate way to detect when something is not correct in the mechanics of your pivot. By doing exercises like the table exercise, you learn to associate certain sensations with the fundamentals of the swing. These sensations will provide you with feedback on what you are doing during the swing. Since the swing happens too quickly for your mind to analyze what you are doing so that you can adjust it while it is in motion, wait until the swing is completed to do your analysis, and make the adjustments on your next shot.

Once you feel comfortable pivoting your left hand, add another piece of masking tape to the tabletop so that the right hand can be added to the exercise.

Add your right hand to the exercise

1. To determine where to place the second piece of masking tape on the tabletop, pivot your left hand so that it is parallel to the side of the table facing you. Place your right hand next to your left hand as if you were gripping a golf club, as in photograph **3.36**. Stick a piece of masking tape on the table to mark the position of your right thumb pad.
2. Take the same address position as you used when you were pivoting your left hand only, as in photograph **3.37**. Place each thumb on its respective piece of masking tape.
3. Pivot both hands together, as in photographs **3.38** and **3.39**. Allow your left hand to dictate the speed of the pivot, and allow the right hand to follow the left. When your right hand follows, your right forearm should move toward the left, just as your left forearm does. At the same time, your right palm and the underside of your right forearm will rotate, and your right elbow will move toward your body. The underside of the right forearm will face upward as it

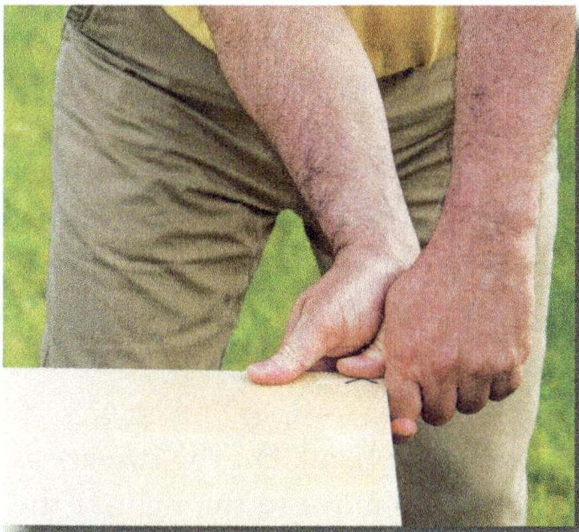

3.36

Place the right hand next to the left hand, and then stick a piece of masking tape on the table to mark the location of the right thumb pad.

3.37

The left and the right thumb pads are on their respective pieces of masking tape.

3.38

Pivot both hands together.

3.39

When you have completed the pivot, both hands will be parallel to the side of the table that faces you.

rotates. As your hands complete the pivot, your right elbow should finish slightly to the left of your right hip. Commit to memory the sensation generated by your hands, wrists, and forearms when both hands pivot together.

AVOID THE DYNAMIC PIVOT POINT

Now that you know how to pivot your hands, let's look at what not to do.

Compare the position of my left hand in photographs **3.40** and **3.41** to its position in photographs **3.28** and **3.34**. Although in photographs **3.40** and **3.41** I have correctly pivoted my left hand through ninety degrees, so that it is parallel to the side of the table facing me, look at the position of my left thumb relative to the masking tape. It has moved well to the right of the tape. In addition, my left forearm, instead of being to the left of the tape, where it is supposed to be, is opposite the tape. This has happened because, as I pivoted my left hand, I allowed my left thumb to move to the right of the masking tape.

This looks very similar to the correct way to pivot your hand, but the two are as different as night and day. Allowing the left thumb to move to the right of the masking tape drastically diminishes your ability to hit flush, crisp shots. When you learn the relationship between the respective sweet spots of the clubface and the ball, which will be discussed later, you will understand why I want you to avoid pivoting the club in this way.

BE CAREFUL: it's very easy to develop the habit of letting your left thumb pad move to the right as you waggle or swing a club. Be on high alert for this fault.

3.40

I allowed my left thumb to move to the right when I pivoted my left hand. This is poor pivoting.

3.41

This shows the final position of the left hand when the left thumb is incorrectly allowed to move off the masking tape.

Use the sensations you learned when you were pivoting your left thumb pad over the piece of masking tape on the table to monitor what you are doing when you are using a club.

Practise Waggling the Club

The set-up

1. Find a level area on the practice range, in your backyard, or in your living room, any place where you have sufficient room to pivot a club through ninety degrees.
2. Drop a golf ball on the ground and position it where you could hit a shot.
3. If you are on the practice range, look around and select a distant target, as in photograph **3.42**. If you are in your living room, imagine a distant target beyond the walls, or select a target close by.
4. Stand facing your target, with the ball between you and the target, as in photograph **3.43**. Establish a target line in your mind.
5. Place two clubs parallel to your target line, one on each side of the ball and several inches away from it. These clubs should be far enough away from the ball that you won't hit them when you pivot the club you are holding. The bottom arrow in photograph **3.43** points to one of these clubs.
6. Place a third club perpendicular to the clubs on the ground and in line with the ball. The top arrow in photograph **3.43** points to this club. I normally

3.42

Select a level lie and a distant target, indicated here by the vertical dotted line.

place the grip end of this club toward the ball, leaving several inches between it and the ball. For waggling, select one of your longer clubs, such as a 3 wood or a 5 wood. It's easier to learn how to pivot or waggle a club when you're using

3.43

Establish your target line in your mind.

a longer club rather than a shorter one, such as a wedge. Note that when these photos were taken, I just used what I had with me.

7. Place the clubhead behind the ball with the clubface perpendicular to the target line, as in photographs **3.44** and **3.45**.
8. Align yourself with your hips and shoulders parallel to the target line in an address position suitable for hitting a straight shot, as in photograph **3.46**.

3.44

Align the clubface perpendicular to the target line.

3.45

A view of the clubface when it is aligned perpendicular to the target line.

3.46

The hips and shoulders are aligned parallel to the target line; this is the position from which to hit a straight shot.

3.47

The left thumb pad is in line with the back half of the ball, exactly where it should be.

9. Check your left thumb position relative to the ball. If you have addressed the ball correctly, your left thumb pad should be in line with the back half of the ball, as in photographs **3.47** and **3.48**. This position of the left thumb pad relative to the back of the ball is important, and you must get it right each time you address the ball. Adjust your address position until your left thumb pad is aligned with the ball correctly.

Pivot the club from the ball to a position parallel to the target line

When you waggle the club away from the ball until it is parallel to the target line, the last three fingers of the left hand apply a force to the club while the left thumb pad pivots about its initial position, as in photograph **3.49**. The combination of this force and the pivoting left thumb pad precisely controls the movement of the clubhead.

1. Initiate the pivot or waggle by moving the last three fingers of your left hand to your left while maintaining the same thumb position that was established when you were addressing the ball. If you maintain the left thumb position as the club pivots, you will exercise precise control over the movement of the

3.48

Initially, the left thumb is in line with the back half of the ball.

3.49

The left thumb pad pivots about its initial position when the club pivots in response to the pressure of the last three fingers against the golf club grip.

clubhead, which is exactly what is demanded when you are hitting a ball. The right hand grips and supports the club, and moves only in response to the movement of the left hand. The right hand does not exert any force to help the left hand pivot the club from the ball to a position parallel to the target line – it is the left hand that bears sole responsibility for the movement of the club.

Think of what happens when you push a door open. You turn the doorknob and push on the door. The door swings open and you enter. Take a bird's-eye view: the force that is applied to one side of the door, the side nearest to you, causes the door to swing open. The door has two sides, so they both move together. The side closest to you moves because you applied a force to it; the other side also moves, but only because it is part of the structure of the door – there was no force applied to it. The same thing happens when you pivot your hands as you waggle a golf club. The left hand initiates the force against the club, whereas the right hand moves because it is part of the structure of the grip.

2. Let the left thumb pad rotate about its position while the last three fingers are pivoting the hand in a clockwise direction (photograph **3.49**). As the left hand pivots, so does the club.

   When you pivot the left hand while gripping a club you are performing the same movement you used when you pivoted your hand while doing the table and masking tape exercise. The only difference is that instead of the left thumb pad rotating over a piece of masking tape, the club waggles to the right as the left thumb pad rotates about a pivot point. Throughout the waggle, it is critical that the left thumb pad maintain its position relative to the back of the golf ball; see photograph **3.50**.

The reason it is so important for the left thumb pad to rotate about a static pivot point is that this is the only way to maintain the position of the clubface relative to the ball, and thus to preserve the alignment of their sweet spots while you are pivoting the club through ninety degrees, until it is parallel to the target line. In fact, a static pivot point preserves the alignment of the sweet spots throughout the whole of the backswing and the downswing. And when the clubface contacts the ball, the sweet spots remain aligned as they were at the start of the backswing. All of this occurs because a static pivot point was used throughout.

Keep the clubhead close to the ground as you pivot the club, as in photograph **3.50**. (Ideally, you should skim the ground with the clubhead, but in these photos I have not done so.) Compare the position of the clubhead in photograph **3.50** with that in photograph **3.51**. If you cock your wrists during the waggle, as in photograph **3.51**, you will lift the clubhead off the ground. There is no need to do this.

3.50

The left thumb remains in its original position, despite the fact that the club has pivoted through ninety degrees to a position parallel to the target line. Ideally, the clubhead should skim the ground throughout the waggle.

When you are learning to waggle a club, it is helpful to notice the path that the clubhead follows along the ground, because it gives you a physical record by which you can assess whether you are waggling your club properly. If the clubhead

3.51

Here, I cocked my wrists as I pivoted the club, and consequently I lifted the clubhead farther above the ground than necessary.

is pivoted correctly, the path you will see is a quarter-circle. We can use a clock analogy again here: this quarter-circle arc starts from the ball (at twelve o'clock), and ends where the clubhead finishes, parallel to the target line (at three o'clock). Tracking the movement of the clubhead through this arc will help you develop a mental picture of the correct clubhead path to use when approaching a ball before the moment of impact.

A plush carpet, a dry sandy beach, or the practice tee (where the grass is a little longer than on the course itself) are ideal surfaces on which to trace out the movement of the clubhead.

3. Continue to pivot the club with your left hand until the club is parallel with the target line, as in photograph **3.50**.

   As you pivot the club from the ball to a position parallel to the target line, there is no need for your hips or shoulders to turn; the only parts of your body that should move are your hands, your wrists, and your forearms.

   The left hand stops pivoting when the club shaft is parallel to the target line. Hold the club in this position momentarily, while the role of the hands reverses. To pivot the clubhead back to the ball, apply force against the club with the right hand, not the left.

Pivot the club back to the ball

1. Push your right hand against the club in the direction of your target line, as in photographs **3.52** and **3.53**.

3.52

To move the clubhead back to the ball, exert force toward the target line using only your right hand.

3.53

The right hand applies force to the club in the direction of the target line.

When it comes time to pivot the club back in the direction of the ball, the force exerted by the right hand will overcome the inertia of the club in its position parallel to the target line. Once you set the club in motion, you'll

3.54

Both hands pivot about the left thumb pad as the clubhead returns to the ball. At the end of the pivot, both hands will be back in their original address position.

need very little force to continue. The left hand will move with the movement of the club. The structure of the grip allows the club to pivot about the left thumb pad while the right hand is providing the force.

2. Stop pivoting the club when the clubhead returns to the back of the ball. When you pivot the club back to the ball you are simulating what happens on the downswing prior to the moment of impact. Pay particular attention to the way both hands pivot about the left thumb as they return to their original address position, as in photograph **3.54**.

3.55

When the hands approach the ball during the downswing, they are parallel to the target line.

3.56

The unwinding of the hips and the shoulders whips the hands around the left thumb pad, and delivers a powerful blow to the ball.

The downswing brings both hands back to their original address position with great speed and force. The shoulders unwind, the arms move rapidly, and the hands pivot about the left thumb pad and swing back to their original position, as in photographs **3.55** and **3.56**. When the hands return to their original address position, the clubhead compresses the ball and produces a well-struck shot. The unwinding of the hips and shoulders contributes to the speed at which the hands pivot about the left thumb. As the shoulders unwind parallel to the target line, the arms are pulled along in the same direction. When the shoulders, arms, and pivoting hands combine to return to their original address position, they constitute a very powerful mechanism for delivering a force to the ball. It is a satisfying experience to feel these mechanics and this structure at work. It is even more deeply satisfying to watch the ball fly with the authority that was imposed on it when these conditions were established at the critical moment of contact. You can often see touring pros watching their shots with great intensity – the "faraway look" in their eyes is a joy to witness.

Maintain a Stationary Position

WHEN YOU WAGGLE THE GOLF CLUB back and forth, the only parts of your body that should move are your hands, your wrists, and your forearms. Your upper arms, between your elbow and your shoulder joint, should remain stationary and close to your upper body during the waggle. When you align your shoulders parallel to the target line, you should feel as if all the action is taking place under them.

If you practise waggling a club in the way I have described it, you will have a front row seat from which to observe, monitor, and adjust your hand action. No one has a better view of your hand action than you do. Although you need a second pair of eyes when you're learning or troubleshooting other aspects of the golf swing, this is not the case when you are learning the hand action of the waggle. When, during the waggle, you isolate the motion of the body from the hand action, you have a wonderfully effective way to learn the most fundamental building block of the golf swing. And if you adopt a static address position, it is easy to learn the hand action of the waggle.

Establish the Correct Path for the Clubhead

IN ORDER FOR THE THE BALL to fly in the direction of the target, the clubhead must be travelling along the target line at the moment it strikes the ball, and the clubface must be perpendicular to the target line at the same moment (see photograph **3.57**).

Because you are standing to one side of the ball, the clubhead will travel along the target line for only a short distance. At the beginning of the movement to pivot the club from the ball to a position parallel to the target line, the clubhead moves

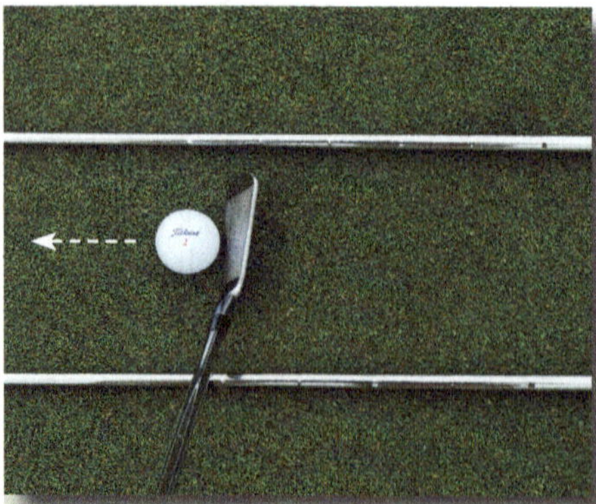

3.57

At the moment of impact, the clubhead must be moving along the target line, and the clubface must be perpendicular to the ball and the target line.

3.58

The clubface remains perpendicular to its arc while the clubhead is moving within the "inside" zone, between you and the target line.

away from the ball on a path along the target line. But then it moves to an area that golfers call "inside the target line" – the zone between your feet and the ball – as the club pivots into the three o'clock position (parallel to the target line). On the downswing, as the club pivots back to the ball, the clubhead arc returns through the "inside" zone, and then travels along the target line as it approaches the ball. As it travels along this path – from twelve o'clock to three o'clock, and then back to twelve o'clock – the clubface should always be perpendicular to the path of the clubhead, as in photograph **3.58**. Correct hand action is responsible for producing all of these conditions. When you are learning and practising the waggle, develop an awareness of these factors by observing and sensing the clubhead in motion.

Back to the Clock Analogy

LET'S USE THE IMAGE OF THE CLOCK again to help us grasp a couple of useful ideas. In photograph **3.59**, I have placed a blue dot on the number 12 to represent the sweet spot of the ball, and another on the tip of the hand to represent the sweet spot of the clubface. But notice that I have made the two dots out of alignment with each other. This is analogous to the situation of a golfer who is only using his eyesight when addressing the ball on the golf course. No matter how hard you try to align the sweet spot of the clubface with the sweet spot of the ball using sight alone, it cannot be done. You can begin the process on the basis of a visual impression, and establish a rough approximation of the alignment, but if you want to fine-tune the alignment you have to use another method.

3.59

In this photograph, the dot on the 12 represents the sweet spot of the ball, and the dot on the tip of the clock hand represents the sweet spot of the clubface. The fact that the two blue dots are out of alignment represents the relationship between the two sweet spots at the moment when the address position is first adopted, and the alignment has been done using sight alone.

Observe what happens when I pivot the clock hand back and forth. I can do so as many times as I like and I am always able to return it and its blue dot back to its original position. I can do this because the clock hand is fixed in length and because I am pivoting it about a fixed pivot point. If I were to align the two blue dots perfectly, I could pivot the clock hand repeatedly and the dots would remain perfectly aligned, as in photographs **3.60** to **3.63**. Similarly, if you could learn a way to align the sweet spots of the clubface and the ball and then pivot the club about a fixed or static pivot point, you could repeat this action successfully every time.

As we see when we compare the golf swing to the clock, if we align the sweet spots at address and the club is pivoted about a fixed pivot point during the backswing, we can preserve the alignment of the sweet spots. You need to be able to pivot the club through ninety degrees, to the point where the club shaft is parallel to the target line. This is because when you're at the top of the backswing, the best position from which to start the downswing is with the club parallel to the target line. Pivoting the club through ninety degrees during the backswing allows you to achieve the correct club position at the top of the backswing.

On the downswing, when your hands are at hip height or perhaps slightly below, the club should be parallel to the target line, as in photograph **3.64**.

The unwinding of the shoulders and hips, together with the force applied against the club by the right hand, pivot the club back to the ball; see photograph **3.65**.

If the pivoting is done correctly, at the moment of impact the sweet spot of the clubface will align with the sweet spot of the ball. If at the same time the clubface is perpendicular to the target line, your shot will fly toward your target in a straight line.

3.60

3.61

3.62

3.63

3.60 - *In this photograph, the dots are properly aligned. The hand remains the same length, and it always pivots about a fixed point.*

3.61 - *Imagine that an arc is being traced as the blue dot on the clock hand moves toward three o'clock. Compare the alignment of the arc to the position of the blue dot at twelve o'clock.*

3.62 - *The longer the arc is, the easier it is to tell whether the blue dot on the clock hand is aligned with the blue dot at twelve o'clock.*

3.63 - *The clock hand continues until it reaches three o'clock; then it returns to twelve o'clock. At that point, we can again determine whether the arc traced by the blue dot on the hand is in alignment with the blue dot at twelve o'clock.*

3.64

When the hands are at hip height, the shaft of the club is parallel to the target line. Notice that for me, the club is parallel when my hands are slightly below my hips.

3.65

The unwinding of the hips and shoulders and the application of force by the right hand pivot the club back to the ball with force and precision.

Align the Sweet Spots

IMAGINE USING A GOLF BALL that has a black line drawn around it. When you place this ball on the target line with the black line aligned with the target line, as in photograph **3.66**, the sweet spot of the ball is a point on the black line directly over the target line. Because each club in your bag has a different amount of loft, the clubface of each one will contact the ball at a different point on the bottom half of the ball. The more loft the club has, the farther down on the ball the club will make contact. If, at the moment of impact, the sweet spot of the clubface hits a point on the black line, it will produce maximum compression of the ball. We call this aligning the sweet spots at the moment of impact.

How do you know whether you have contacted the ball with the sweet spot of the clubface? Well, if you have ever contacted a ball with the toe of the clubface, you will have experienced the feeling you might have if you hit a twenty-pound ball, and you have had your club turn in your hands. At the other extreme, if you have ever hit the ball on the hosel of the clubhead, your hands will have had to absorb the vibrations of the club shaft – an unpleasant experience at best, and one that you need experience only once and you'll remember it forever! When you contact the ball on the sweet spot of the clubface, though, the ball feels weightless, because it absorbs the force applied to it as it compresses. Also, at the moment of impact the clubhead is balanced, so the force applied to the sweet spot of the clubface by the ball does not require any increase in grip pressure to prevent the club from turning in your hands.

Your goal is to achieve maximum compression of the ball at the moment of impact by applying force at a point along the target line. If you achieve maximum compression, the ball will travel the maximum distance. Another reason the alignment of the sweet spots is important is that it gives the maximum amount of spin to the ball, which in turn gives maximum definition to the ball's flight. When a professional golfer hits a ball, it flies a course that a crosswind can scarcely affect. When the sweet spots are aligned at the moment of impact, the grooves of the clubface impart sufficient spin to the ball that it will fly with authority, and with the characteristics defined by the address position.

The sweet spot of the clubface is not explicitly marked on the surface of most clubs, nor should it be. It is usually a little off-centre, more toward the hosel than the toe of the clubface. As a golfer, you learn the location of the sweet spot of the clubface simply by hitting good shots and bad shots until you have developed a mental history of the subject. This mental history develops into an internal sense

3.66

The black line on the ball is placed vertically directly over the white target line. Contact is made on the black line below the red line at a point that is determined by the loft of the clubface that is being used to strike the ball.

of how far to stand from the ball in order to align the sweet spot of any particular clubface with the sweet spot of the ball. This internal sense allows you to make much finer adjustments through the sense of feel than you could ever achieve by sight. For this reason it serves no useful purpose to display the sweet spot on the surface of a clubface.

Align the clubface to the ball

1. Stand behind the ball, facing your target. With the ball in the foreground and the target in the distance, choose your target line (photograph **3.67**). Select a reference object on the target line.
2. Continue to face the ball, but move from behind it to beside it.
3. Hold the club in your right hand while resting your upper right arm against your chest. Step toward the target line with your right foot, close enough to the ball that you are able to place the clubhead behind the ball, with the clubface perpendicular to your reference object. See photographs **3.68** and **3.69**.

   When you step forward with your right foot, your right shoulder and hip also move closer to the target line. This leaves your left foot, your shoulder, and your hip farther from the target line, as in photograph **3.69**. When you do this, your body points in the direction of your reference object, which is exactly what you want. This position gives you the best view from which to align the clubface perpendicular to the reference object and, thus, perpendicular to your distant target. When the right shoulder is closer to the target line than the left shoulder, we say that the shoulders are open. At this point I bring my left hand to the club to begin my left-hand grip, which will bring my shoulders into alignment with the target line.

3.67

Stand behind the ball, with the ball in the foreground and the target in the distance.

3.68

Stand beside the ball.

4. Once the clubface is perpendicular to the line between the ball and your reference object (see photograph **3.70**), align the sweet spot of the clubface with the sweet spot of the ball. You may have to move closer to or farther away from the target line to alter the position of the clubface relative to the centre

3.69

Step toward the target line with your right foot so that you can place the clubhead behind the ball.

3.70

The clubface is behind the ball and perpendicular to the line joining the ball and the reference object (the tee).

of the ball. Do so by moving your right foot, and keep your upper right arm against your upper torso.

Initially, use your eyes to align the sweet spots. Additional adjustments will inevitably be required to fine-tune the alignment. I like to think of the old radios, which had two knobs for tuning, one for coarse adjustments and the other for fine adjustments. Aligning the sweet spots by sight is analogous to turning the coarse-adjustment knob. Aligning the sweet spots by feel is analogous to turning the fine-adjustment knob.

Do not spend a lot of time using your sense of sight to align the sweet spots. Once you have taken your stance and have aligned your body to the target

3.71

This is the position of your feet when you place the clubhead behind the ball. Align the clubface perpendicular to the line joining the ball and the reference object, take your grip, and align your shoulders parallel to the target line.

3.72

Position the toe of your left shoe directly below your shoulders, align your left instep with the left side of your torso, and then turn your left foot twenty-two degrees toward your target.

line, you can concentrate on making the fine adjustments needed to align the clubface to the ball. I go through this process each time I hit a shot – it is a permanent feature of my pre-shot routine.

5. Once the clubface is perpendicular to the target line and the sweet spots are roughly aligned, take your left-hand grip, while continuing to hold the club with your right hand. Do not let the clubface move out of position. As you bring your left hand toward the club, allow your left shoulder to move slightly, so that it is the same distance from the target line as your right shoulder. Once your left-hand grip is complete, take your right-hand grip. Be conscious of keeping your shoulders parallel to your target line (it's very easy to neglect this detail).

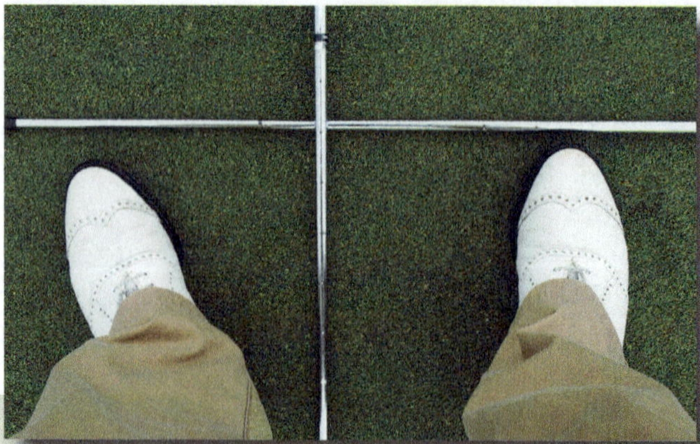

3.73

Position your right foot so that it is perpendicular to the target line, the toe of your shoe is directly below your shoulder, and your instep is in line with the right side of your upper torso.

When both your hands are on the club and your shoulders are parallel to the target line, it is time to adjust your stance, which at this point should look like the one in photographs **3.69** and **3.71**, because when you placed the clubhead behind the ball (step 3, page 125), you probably had to step toward the target line with your right foot. Now you need to position the left foot.

6. Transfer your weight to your right foot so that you can lift your left foot off the ground. Move your left foot forward and slightly to your left so that your left toe is directly below your left shoulder. Position your left instep parallel to the left side of your torso, and then turn your left foot out approximately twenty-two degrees toward your target, as in photograph **3.72**.
7. With your left foot in position, put all your weight on your left foot and move your right foot until the toe of your right shoe is directly below your right shoulder and your right instep is aligned with the right side of your upper torso, as in photograph **3.73**. Place your right foot perpendicular to your target line.

   Adjust your stance, if necessary, so that your knees, hips, and shoulders are all parallel to the target line. You may want to adjust the width of your stance so that it feels more comfortable.

   From the good and bad golf shots you have hit, you have learned where the sweet spot is on the clubface. Now you're ready to align the sweet spot of the clubface to the sweet spot of the ball.
8. Look at the ball and waggle the club continuously between the ball, at twelve o'clock, and the three o'clock position parallel to the target line. As you waggle the club, adjust the distance you stand from the target line until your instincts tell you the alignment of the sweet spots cannot be improved.

HOW I ALIGN THE SWEET SPOTS

From the moment I first place the clubhead behind the ball to the moment I have the sweet spots aligned, the mental image I have of the sweet spot of the clubface changes significantly. When I place the clubhead behind the ball, I picture the sweet spots on the clubface and the ball as being about the size of a quarter, as in photographs **3.74** and **3.75**.

I've made the blue dots large in order to indicate that at this point the margin of error is so great that it's safe to assume that the sweet spots are out of alignment. As I waggle the clubhead back and forth, I have a mental image of an arc the width of a quarter that is traced by the sweet spot of the clubhead. See photographs **3.76** to **3.79**.

Let's take a moment here to revisit our clock analogy. When I pivoted the clock hand back and forth, the blue dots on the hand formed a solid arc. Suppose you had a way of moving the pivot point of the clock hand either closer to the number twelve or farther away from it. You would still be able to pivot the hand back and

3.74

The blue dot on the clubface represents my mental image of the sweet spot of the clubface.

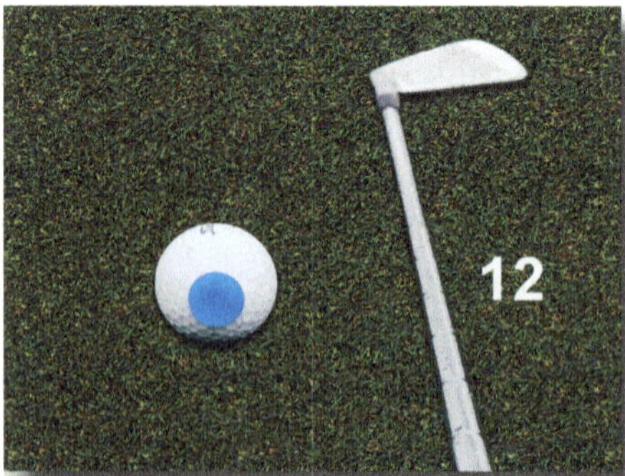

3.75

I have the same mental image of the sweet spot of the ball as I have of the sweet spot of the clubface.

forth, but the dot on the hand would no longer be in perfect alignment with the dot on the number twelve. The solution would be to change the location of the pivot point. The same situation can arise when you are aligning the sweet spots of the clubface and the ball. In this case, you change the location of the pivot point by adjusting the distance between your feet and the target line.

As I improve the alignment of the sweet spots by adjusting the distance I stand from the target line, I imagine the sweet spots of the clubface and the ball getting smaller, as in photograph **3.80**. As a result, the width of the imaginary blue arc gets narrower and narrower, as in photograph **3.81**. This process continues until I have the sweet spots perfectly aligned. When they are perfectly aligned, the blue dots disappear from my mind, as does my mental image of the blue arc. No further adjustments are required, so I move on to my takeaway and backswing.

Since you are not allowed to move the ball without incurring a penalty, the only way you can bring the sweet spots into alignment is by changing the position of the clubface in relation to the ball. To do this, you must adjust the distance between your feet and the target line. With time and practice, you will develop an address position in which your arms will hang in the same position for each club you swing. Do not change the position of the clubface relative to the ball by changing the position of your arms. Keep the same address position for all clubs, and when you need to change the position of the clubface relative to the ball, do so by adjusting the distance between your feet and the target line.

When you are on the practice tee to improve your ball striking, I recommend that you use a club that has a small sweet spot. Use a blade iron instead of a cavity back iron. Take it to the driving range and use the ideas I have given you for

3.76

I begin to pivot the club to get a sense of how to fine-tune the alignment of the sweet spots. Do I need to move closer to or farther away from the target line?

3.77

The clubhead begins to move inside the target line, creating a long arc that I can use as I assess the alignment of the sweet spots.

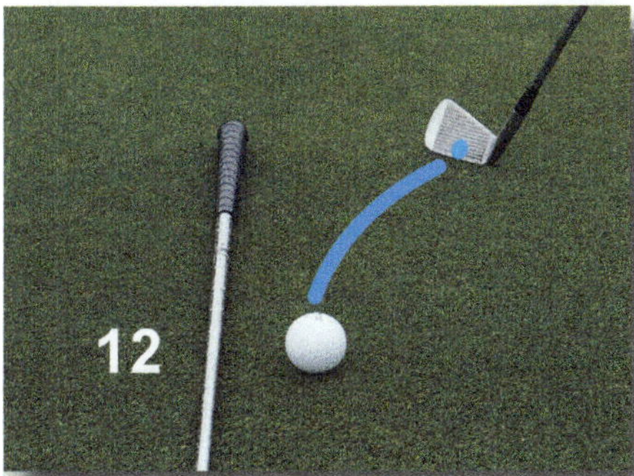

3.78

The clubhead moves along the arc created by pivoting the club about the left thumb pad, which remains static. When you visualize the arc created by the blue dot you are able to discern what adjustments you need to make in order to align the sweet spots.

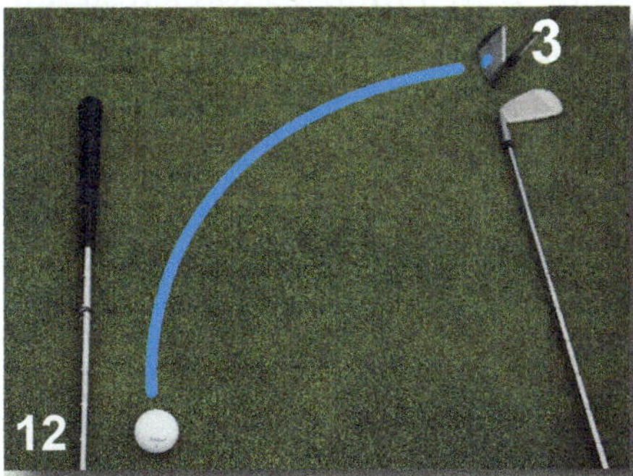

3.79

The full arc between the ball and the clubhead at the three o'clock position.

pivoting a club and aligning the sweet spots. As you improve your ball striking you can go back to your cavity backs for the extra assurance they provide. I have often thought that it would be a good idea for a golf club manufacturer to produce a training club with an intentionally small sweet spot. If the ideas of this lesson were applied to such a club, I am certain your shots would improve. It would be a great way to fine-tune your ability to align the sweet spots.

3.80

As I fine-tune the alignment of the sweet spots, I imagine the sweet spot on the ball to be getting smaller.

3.81

As the blue dots get smaller, the blue arc gets narrower.

Pivot Your Hands, Don't Roll Them

I HAVE PLACED TWO coloured stripes, one red and one yellow, on the clock hand in photograph **3.82**. I am now going to pivot the clock hand ninety degrees, to three o'clock.

When I pivot the clock hand ninety degrees, to three o'clock, as in photograph **3.83**, both coloured stripes remain visible.

3.82

There is a red stripe and a yellow stripe on the top surface of the clock's hand.

3.83

As I pivot the clock hand from twelve o'clock to three o'clock, both coloured stripes remain visible.

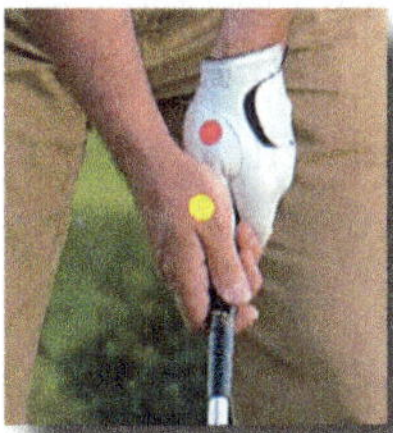

3.84

The red dot on my left hand represents the red stripe on the clock hand. The yellow dot on my right hand represents the yellow stripe on the clock hand.

The red stripe corresponds to my left hand and the yellow one corresponds to my right hand. I have placed a red dot on my left hand and a yellow dot on my right hand. As you can see in photograph **3.84**, both dots can be seen when I'm in my address position.

3.85

When you pivot your hands, never lose sight of the red and yellow dots. Here, the dots were visible to me while I pivoted my hands a full ninety degrees, which confirms that I pivoted my hands correctly.

If I pivot my hands properly, in the way I have described throughout this chapter, I will never lose sight of these dots. When I have pivoted the club to a position parallel to the target line I should still be able to see these dots, as in photograph **3.85**. The fact that I can still see both dots confirms that I have not rolled my hands.

The amateur golfer who does not know how to use his hands has a tendency to roll his hands on the backswing. What does rolling your hands look like? Let's go back to the clock for a minute. Rolling my hands would be analogous to rotating the clock hand clockwise, and consequently hiding the red and yellow stripes seen in photographs **3.82** and **3.83**, at the same time as I am pivoting it from twelve o'clock to three o'clock. In terms of the human body, rolling your hands means twisting your left wrist so that the back of the left hand faces upward. Typically, the amateur golfer rolls his hands because he has no understanding that he should pivot them.

Another way of thinking about it is to compare rolling your hands with giving the volume knob of an old radio a quick clockwise turn. After doing that could you give the same knob a quick counterclockwise turn back to exactly where it was? The answer is no. Here we have the difference between the professional golfer and the amateur golfer – the amateur golfer tries to do the impossible, whereas the professional golfer contents himself with mastering the possible.

Pivoting your hands in the manner I have described in this chapter is a structured method of returning the clubface back to the ball so that it is in exactly the same position as it was when you set up your address. The proper grip pivots the club about the left thumb pad, while the unwinding of the shoulders makes the arms move parallel to the target line. The end result is that the clubface is perpendicular to the ball at the moment of impact and is moving along the target line – the two conditions necessary for hitting an accurate shot. These conditions cannot be consistently replicated if you roll your hands.

The Professional Waggle

YOU WILL NOT SEE professional golfers waggle the golf club from twelve o'clock to three o'clock; normally they do an abbreviated version of this arc. Nonetheless, they pivot the clubhead along the same path as the one I have been describing. The length of the waggle varies with the individual golfer.

Mike Weir does something unique: first he makes sure that the ball and the club are on the same plane (see photograph **3.86**), and then he positions his clubhead behind the ball (see photograph **3.87**) and starts his backswing. This is a clever check to perform. I receive feedback telling me that the ball and the club are on the same plane about a quarter of the way into the downswing, when the left arm is parallel to the ground, whereas Mike Weir double-checks this before starting

3.86

In this Mike Weir signature move, I swing my arms and club into this position to confirm that the club and the ball will remain on the same plane. The white line represents an imagined extension of the shaft to ground level, where it meets the ball on the target line. If the golfer begins his downswing from the proper position at the top of the backswing, he will sense that his left arm, too, is on the same plane as the ball and the club.

3.87

Confident now that the club and the ball are on the same plane, I position my clubhead behind the ball and start my backswing.

his swing. Is this necessary? Not really. If you use the same address position for each club and have your sweet spots aligned, you can be confident that the ball and the club will be on the same plane.

I find Mike Weir's habit interesting, because it shows that you can learn something about the swing by watching the professional golfer. In fact, each time a professional swings a golf club he is demonstrating how it is done. The barrier to entry to the ranks of the professionals is the ability to convert what your eyes see to logical thought – not an easy process. It is what a scientist does when he tries to make sense of experimental data.

Ted Williams, the legendary player for the Boston Red Sox and a fishing acquaintance of mine, was like this with salmon fishing. Although he had spent much of his life on the river, he kept asking questions about the salmon, trying to learn more and more, even into his mid-eighties. Hypothesizing and seeking answers is an age-old human quality, and it has served us well. I respected Ted for this quality, and I believe that it serves a golfer well in learning the golf swing.

4 | Adding the Shoulder Turn

UP TO THIS POINT, YOU HAVE learned how to use your hands correctly while standing in an address position with your shoulders parallel to the target line. You can waggle the golf club through ninety degrees and position it parallel to the target line. You are able to pivot the clubhead back to the ball on a path that is inside the target line – the zone between you and the ball – an ability that is critical for hitting accurate shots. You know how to return the clubface to a position perpendicular to the target line while allowing the clubhead to travel along the target line in its final approach back to the ball. All of this is possible because you know how to use your hands and arms, and you recognize the importance of aligning your shoulders parallel to the target line as you address the ball.

Coordinate Your Shoulder Turn with Your Hand Action

DURING THE DOWNSWING (the sequence of movements leading up to the moment of impact), you must position your shoulders so that they are parallel to the target line at the moment of impact. If you are unable to do this, your shoulder turn will interfere with your hand action and prevent you from using your hands in the way you have learned in this book. Therefore, the next step is for me to teach you how to coordinate your shoulder turn so that your shoulders are parallel to the target line at the moment of impact and your hands can function as they should.

Consider my own experience: after I learned how to use my hands correctly while standing in the address position, I found that I couldn't use them in the same way during my swing. During my swing, my hands tried to approach the ball from inside the target line, but were prevented from doing so because my shoulders were not parallel to it. I realized that my arms were moving in the same direction as my shoulders – across the target line rather than parallel to it. My shoulders were not parallel to the target line, so my arms were not moving parallel to the target line either. After experiencing these conflicting sensations for a week, I realized that my shoulder turn was interfering with the correct functioning of my hands. I needed to find a way to position my shoulders parallel to the target line at the moment of impact in such a way that they wouldn't interfere with my hand action. By pure chance, I found a way to do this by using a modified version of the Paul Runyan chipping technique.

I had purchased a copy of Runyan's book, *The Short Way to Lower Scoring*, and had begun to apply his technique to my putting and chipping game. The Paul Runyan chipping technique is a stiff-wristed technique performed by the arms and shoulders only, and it did not take me long to recognize that there was something significant about it. As I honed my mastery of Runyan's technique around the green, I decided to see what would happen if I tried it on longer shots. When I did so, I saw a need to modify it slightly – I needed to cock my wrists. When I did that, I was able to make three-quarter swings using a full shoulder turn, and when I did so I discovered an effective way to monitor what my shoulders were doing and make the appropriate adjustments. I found it easy to adjust my shoulder turn so that my shoulders were parallel to the target line at the moment of impact, just as they were when I waggled the club, as I described in Chapter 3.

If the shoulders are parallel to the target line in the last moments before impact, the clubhead moves on a path that begins inside the target line, and joins the target line just prior to the moment of impact. The clubface pivots back to the ball so that it is perpendicular to the target line at the moment of impact, thereby achieving the conditions for hitting a straight and accurate shot. Since discovering this method of adjusting my shoulders, I have never had to alter my shoulder turn in any other way. In my opinion, it is by far the simplest and most effective way to teach yourself how to use your shoulders. The Runyan chipping technique is one you should not ignore, so we will now take a short detour to learn it and my modified version of it. If you master these chipping techniques you will learn how to turn your shoulders properly in both your long game and your short game.

PAUL RUNYAN

Paul Runyan was a PGA touring professional in the 1930s and 1940s who developed a reputation among his colleagues for his superb short game. After retiring from professional competition he wrote *The Short Way to Lower Scoring*, in which he explains his short game technique. I recommend that you read it and use Runyan's techniques. Strangely, despite his reputation and the knowledge he offers, his technique is still not widely used by the golfing public. I suspect that most amateur golfers are unaware of the virtues of his method. Having used Runyan's technique myself, I can assure you that it is well worth learning and using, and I find it very disturbing that for most people his knowledge sits idle in obscurity. I know of no other way to monitor and adjust your shoulder turn and coordinate it with your hand action than to use my modified version of the Paul Runyan technique, and I am very pleased to offer it to you. For me it provides clear, direct feedback that I can use quickly and easily.

THE PAUL RUNYAN CHIPPING TECHNIQUE

The set-up for the firm-wristed chipping stroke

1. Crouch down behind the ball and face the hole you want to chip to. This lowers your eyes to green level so that you can see the slope of the green.

Having judged the slope of the green, plan how hard and high you want to hit your chip shot. Once you have these two factors figured out, select the line along which you want the ball to roll to the hole. Next, pick a spot on the green where the ball should land in order for it to roll along the line you have chosen. The spot on the green where you want to land the ball is your target. This is all that you yourself can control; once the ball hits the putting green, it's under the green's control. Your target line is a line between your ball and the spot on the green where you want your ball to land. Pick out a reference object on the target line a couple of feet in front of the ball, and use it to position the clubface perpendicular to the target line. Or, if you like, you might want to do what I do, which is to place a couple of clubs on either side of my target line, as in photograph **4.00,** when I practise my chipping.

2. Stand up and move to the side of the ball; position your head so that your eyes are directly over your target line and the ball. How do you know whether your eyes are over the target line? Hang a club from the bridge of your nose, as in photograph **4.01** – if the club points to the ball, you know that your eyes are over the target line. If the club points to the ground on your side of the target line, you are standing too far away (this is the most common mistake); if it points to the other side, you are standing too close. If your eyes are not over the target line when you chip – a common fault among amateurs – your aim will be off.
3. Place the clubhead behind the ball so that the clubface is perpendicular to the line joining the ball and your reference object. Have the toe of the club resting on the ground and the heel off the ground, as in photograph **4.02**.

4.00

I crouch behind the ball to determine the slope of the green, the spot on the green where I want the ball to land, and the line that I want the ball to roll along on its way to the hole.

4.01

Confirm that your eyes are over the target line by hanging a club from between your eyes. If the club is pointing at the top of the ball, your eyes are in the correct position.

It may seem a bit strange to have the heel of the club off the ground and the toe touching it, but this is what you need to do in order to maintain the position of your eyes over the target line.

4. Align yourself so that your feet, hips, and shoulders are all parallel to the target line. Position the toe of your left foot directly opposite the ball – or, if you need to hit down on the ball a bit more, stand with the ball a little farther to the right, as I've done in photograph **4.03**. Your stance should be wide enough that the outside edge of each shoe is in line with the side of your upper torso, and your weight should be distributed evenly between both feet. Position the club grip slightly to the left of the clubface, but keep the clubface perpendicular to the target line so that you will contact the ball cleanly and crisply.

4.02

Hold the club upright, with the toe touching the ground and the heel off the ground, so that you can stand close to the target line.

4.03

The toes of the shoes, the knees, the hips, and the shoulders all line up parallel to the target line. Normally the ball is opposite the big toe of the left shoe, but if you want to hit down on the ball a little more than usual, move your feet to the left.

Before going any further, you need to learn the arm positions for the Paul Runyan chipping technique, and the reverse overlap golf grip. The reverse overlap grip is commonly used for putting and chipping. Read the sections below on the Position of the Arms and Position of the Hands before proceeding to step 5.

POSITION OF THE ARMS

The traditional chipping method uses the same address position as you would use if you were preparing to hit a full shot, but with a few modifications to the

4.04

When the club is upright and you're standing close enough to the target line to look directly over it, you have to bend your left arm to place your hands on the club.

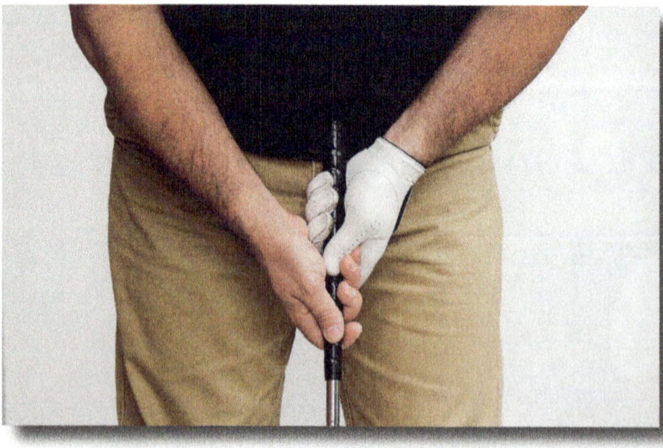

4.05

Position your forearms at about forty-five degrees to the club shaft and point the underside of your forearms upward at the same angle. Grip down on the club as needed.

stance. Normally, an open stance is used for chipping; that is, the right foot is placed closer to the target line than the left foot. The weight is mainly on the left side, and the stance is narrowed to a comfortable width. The traditional chipping method uses a straight left arm, which requires you to stand away from the target line. This, in turn, prevents you from looking directly down at the ball.

Paul Runyan's firm-wristed chipping technique requires you to stand close enough to the target line that you are able to look directly down on your target line and the ball. To do this, place the club in an upright position with the toe of the clubhead touching the ground while the heel is off the ground. To grip the club in this position, bend your left arm and grip down on the club grip. See photograph **4.04**.

4.06

From the perspective of someone beside you and just inside the target line, the club grip is hidden by the left forearm, and the right forearm is in line with the left forearm.

The upper portion of each arm presses lightly against the upper torso for support. The forearms bend at the elbow so that the underside of each forearm faces upward at about a forty-five degree angle, and each forearm makes about a forty-five degree angle with the club, as in photograph **4.05**. The forearms and the club should all be in line with each other. If the club shaft were extended to your elbows, someone standing just inside the target line looking back at you would not see it, because your forearms would hide it from their view (see photograph **4.06**).

THE POSITION OF THE HANDS

For a stiff-wristed chipping technique such as Runyan's, the placement of the hands on the club facilitates the correct position of the forearms – facing upwards at forty-five degrees – so the palms of your hands grip the club facing upward at forty-five degrees too, as is shown in photograph **4.05**.

We will use the reverse overlapping grip. Since you may not be familiar with this grip, I will explain how it is put together, and then demonstrate how to use it.

For this grip, the left index finger overlaps the right little finger somewhat diagonally, as in photograph **4.07**. The tip of the left index finger is more or less between the knuckles of the right little finger and the right ring finger.

To achieve this overlap, separate the left thumb from the palm to create a gap. For chipping it is not critical that we close this gap; since we do not take a full

4.07

4.08

4.07 - *The left index finger overlaps the right little finger, with the tip of the left finger placed between the right little finger and the right ring finger.*

4.08 - *Notice that the right little finger and part of the right ring finger are in the gap between the left thumb and the palm. This gap allows the left hand to get close enough to the right hand to overlap it.*

swing, there is no risk of having the club slide into the gap between the left thumb and palm at the top of the backswing. For the reverse overlap grip, the right little finger and part of the right ring finger fill this gap (as in photograph **4.08**), allowing the left hand to overlap the right hand with the left index finger.

We now continue with the set-up

5. With the club in its upright position, the club grip slightly to the left of the clubface, and your palms open and facing upward, slide your hands into position, as in photograph **4.09**. The left hand slides under the club shaft at an angle that is equal but opposite to the angle of the right hand.

   Depending on which club you have chosen to chip with (I chip with every iron, right up to a 1-iron), you may have to place your right hand below the club grip. Overlap the left index finger over the right little finger as you slide your hands under the club. For the right hand, place the club shaft across the segment of the little finger that is closest to the palm, and across the middle segment of the right index finger. For the left hand, place the club shaft across the segment of the little finger that is closest to the palm, and across the knuckles of the two middle fingers that are closest to the palm.

6. Imagine a clock face attached to the butt end of the club, with twelve o'clock in exact alignment with the clubface. Wrap both hands around the club shaft simultaneously, placing each thumb pad on the club grip. Close the gap

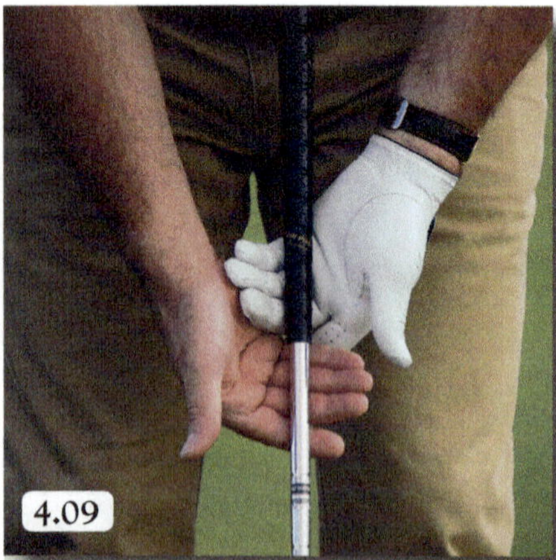

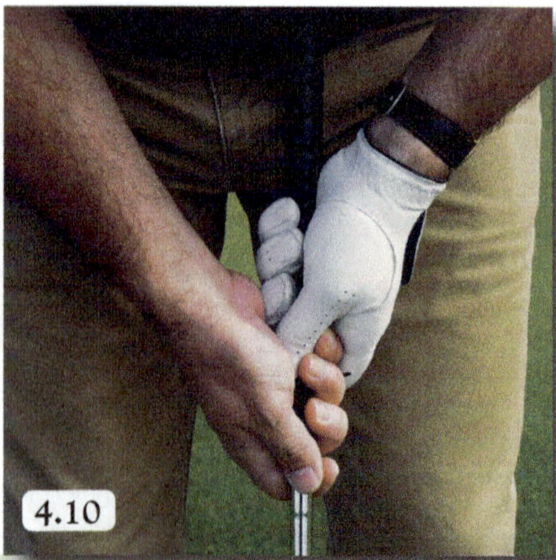

4.09 - *When reading my instructions above, it will be helpful to take note of which parts of the hands the club crosses over. Also, notice that my right hand is placed somewhat below the club grip – how far below will vary, depending on what club you are using to chip with.*

4.10 - *The completed grip, with the left hand and arm providing an equal and opposite force to the right hand and arm.*

between your right thumb and palm, wrap your right hand around the club shaft, and place your right thumb pad at one o'clock (from the view of someone holding the club). Remember that only about half of the right thumb pad contacts the club – the half closest to twelve o'clock will probably not do so. As for the left hand, wrap it around the club shaft so you can place your left thumb pad on the club grip at eleven o'clock (from the view of someone holding the club).

Your completed grip should look like the one shown in photograph **4.10**. With both hands on the club in this way, you should sense that both hands and both arms are supplying equal but opposite forces to the club. If not, adjust your grip as necessary until you achieve this feeling. The back of each hand should be on almost the same plane as its forearm. In this position, the wrists are locked, and any hinging of the wrists is unlikely to occur.

Now that you know how to set up for the Paul Runyan chipping technique, I suggest that you take some time to practise chipping, using this technique.

If you make correct contact with the ball when you are chipping or putting, the ball will roll across the green as if there is no stopping it, and the shot will hold its line very well. Incorrect contact with the ball causes it to lose its speed very quickly, and the shot has a hard time holding its line. When you first start using the Paul Runyan method, I expect that your ball will not roll as it should. Keep practising – with patience, you will learn how to make it work.

Here is a quick tip to speed your progress. Whenever you move the clubhead away from the ball, do so before you move your hands, arms, and shoulders. This

4.11

In the address position the clubhead is, of course, to the left of my right elbow.

4.12

The first good sign: the clubhead reaches the position of my right elbow before my hands do.

4.13

The second good sign: the clubhead passes my right elbow before my hands do. On full shots, this really helps the sequencing of the backswing.

applies to putting, chipping, pitching, and hitting full shots, and it also applies to the Paul Runyan technique. By moving the clubhead first, you begin the proper sequence of hand, arm, and shoulder movements, and that will make a world of difference to how well you contact the ball.

Let's see this in action. In the address position (photograph **4.11**), notice that my clubhead is to the left of my right elbow. When I start my takeaway, I push the clubhead away from the ball with my left hand. I am in no hurry to let my right elbow move. As the clubhead moves away from the ball, it moves along the target line, and then, as my shoulders begin to turn, slightly to the inside of the target line.

By the time the clubhead has moved approximately a foot from the ball, it is even with my right elbow, as in photograph **4.12**, and beyond that point it will pass my right elbow, as in photograph **4.13**. These are signs that the clubhead has moved first and my hands, arms, and shoulders have followed in sequence. This is the correct way to sequence your backswing, and it improves your chances of generating the proper sequence of events during your downswing.

MY MODIFICATION OF THE RUNYAN METHOD

Paul Runyan advises you to move the clubhead straight back from the ball along the target line, and then back again along the same route to contact the ball; see photographs **4.14** and **4.15**. This is very much like the often-quoted image of a pendulum swinging back and forth.

My modification of the Paul Runyan technique allows the clubface to open as my clubhead moves away from the ball. In photograph **4.16** you can see the clubface opening up after it has moved only a couple of inches from the ball. The farther I move the clubhead away from the ball, the more the clubface opens up; see photograph **4.17**. I want the clubface to open so that it remains perpendicular to the arc it is moving along. I don't worry about making sure that the clubface returns to a position perpendicular to the target line at the moment of impact, because I know it will do so – all I have to do is move the club the same distance back to the ball and the clubface will return to its original position.

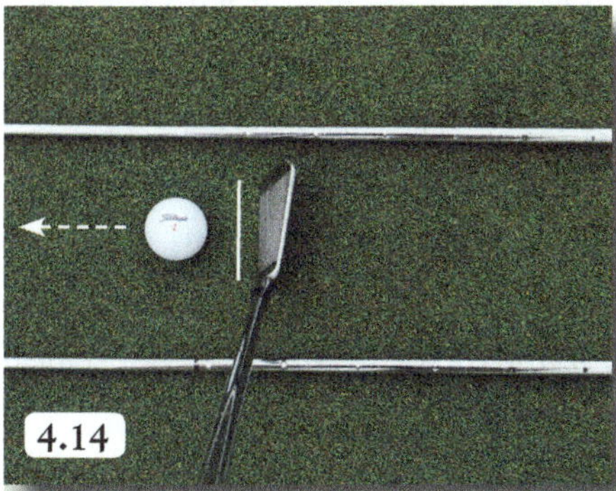

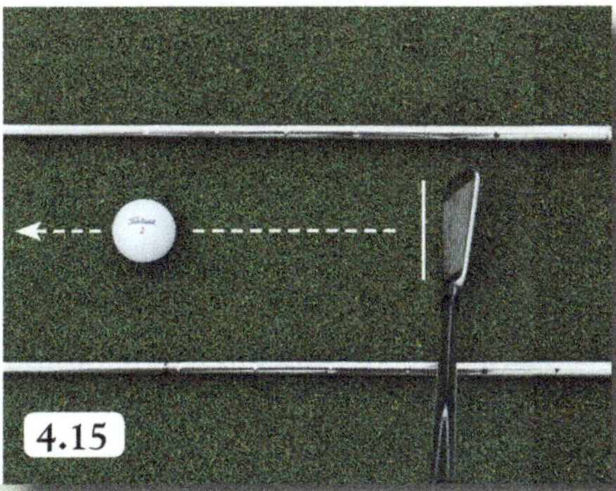

4.14 - *The Runyan technique: the clubhead moves straight back from the ball with the leading edge of the clubface perpendicular to the target line.*

4.15 - *The Runyan technique: when the clubhead is a foot away from the ball, there is very little opening up of the clubface.*

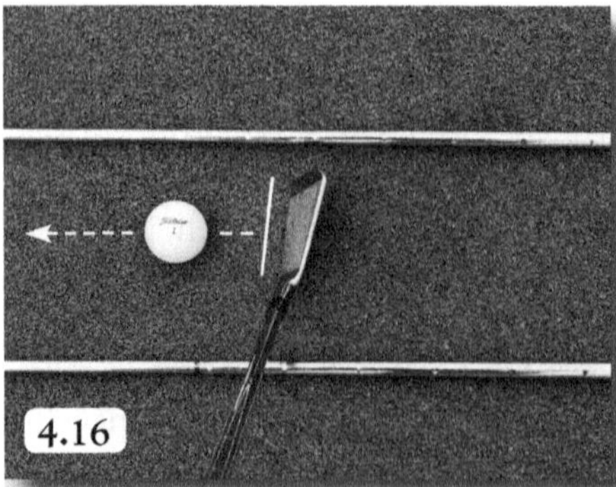

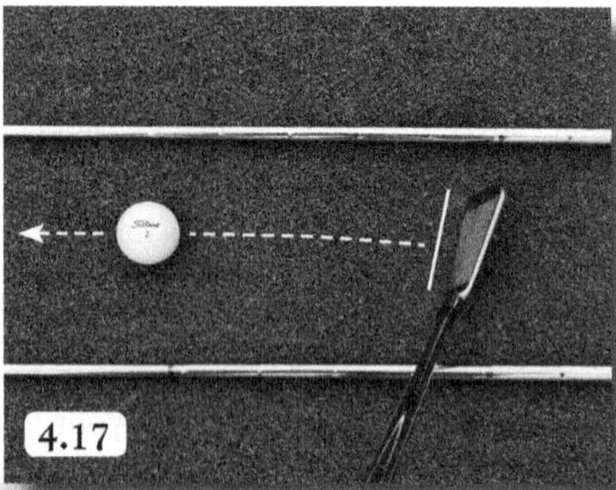

4.16 - *My modification of the Runyan technique: the clubface begins to open ever so slightly after moving only a few inches.*

4.17 - *My modification of the Runyan technique: the clubface is noticeably open, but perpendicular to its arc.*

I abandoned the pendulum approach when I realized that it was impeding my putting and chipping strokes. My version of the putting and chipping stroke is the Paul Runyan technique combined with the opening and closing of the Bobby Jones putting stroke. For me this combination allows the ball to roll off the putter very softly, exactly what you need if you want to maintain control when you are putting fast greens. I could never achieve this quality of putt when I used the straight back-and-forth pendulum image.

Back in the early 1970s, the editors of *Golf Digest* magazine published a book called *All About Putting*. The first chapter describes Bobby Jones's putting stroke. The technique struck a chord with me, and when I combined it with the Paul Runyan method I discovered my own putting stroke. I stand firmly in the camp of those who open and close the clubface. Whether I should or should not is another matter. It's not for me to decide what is best for the golfing population as a whole.

It appears to me that Lorne Roberts, a former PGA touring professional, uses a pendulum putting stroke, and he rolls it as well as is humanly possible. I am left to describe what works for me. For yourself, you will have to try both techniques and go with what works.

PRACTISE HITTING SOME STIFF-WRISTED SHOTS

Once you feel comfortable using the Paul Runyan chipping stroke, try hitting some longer shots. Using the same set-up as was described above to hit chip shots, place a ball on a tee and, starting with the clubhead behind the ball, make a mini-backswing. Swing your arms and turn your shoulders until the club is parallel to the target line and more or less parallel to the ground, as in photograph **4.19**. Then push off your right foot to start your mini-downswing and try to hit the ball fifty to seventy-five yards.

The object of this exercise is to learn how to position the club parallel to the target line. Since your wrists are locked, the only way to do so is by moving your arms and shoulders. For every shot that you hit, the club should be parallel to the target line when it is at hip height, which occurs twice – during your backswing and then again during your downswing. That's the only way to generate any amount of power. If you do not have the club parallel to the target line at these points in your swing, you won't be able to hit it very far.

As you practise this exercise, you will quickly adjust, and learn how to position the club parallel to the target line at hip height. On your first few attempts, I expect you'll be out of position and make a feeble pass at the ball. This is normal. When you learn to position the club parallel to the target line at hip height, you will make a more powerful pass.

No swing that I've seen exemplifies this quality better than that of Tom Kite, another PGA touring professional. You can see that he knows how to move the club through ninety degrees on both the backswing and the downswing.

Practise the Runyan set-up

1. Select a 7-iron or a 5-iron and place a ball on a tee.
2. Choose a target fifty to seventy-five yards away.
3. Establish a target line.
4. Address the ball using the Paul Runyan set-up for chipping. Widen your stance sufficiently to maintain your balance as you hit these shots, as in photograph **4.18**.
5. Push the clubhead away from the ball along the target line, using your left hand and moving your shoulders and arms together as a unit. Throughout the backswing keep your wrists stiff and your arms bent, just as they were in the address position. The combination of stiff wrists and bent arms takes the hands out of the swing and focuses your attention on your shoulder turn. This is exactly what you want for this exercise.

   At hip height, the club should be parallel to the target line and the ground, as in photograph **4.19**. This is a long enough backswing for this exercise.

   As you turn your shoulders and move your arms, you should feel your hands moving along an arc just as the clock did when it moved from twelve o'clock to three o'clock. Think of a door swinging through ninety degrees as it is being pushed open. The left hand is analogous to the side of the door on which the pressure is being applied. The right hand is analogous to the other side of the

4.18

Set up with the ball on a tee, and use a slightly wider stance than what is used for the Paul Runyan chipping set-up.

door – it moves because it is part of the door, not because it is being pushed. The push against the club by the left hand applies a force to the left shoulder that causes both shoulders to pivot about the spine. The right shoulder moves in response to the force applied to the left shoulder. And, lastly, as you make your shoulder turn and move your arms and hands, you should feel more weight being transferred to your right foot.

6. When the club is parallel to the target line at hip height, transfer your weight from the right side to the left by pushing off with your right foot (see

4.19

The club is parallel to the target line and more or less parallel to the ground at hip height.

4.20

Start the downswing by transferring your weight from the right side to the left side.

photograph **4.20**). Your right foot is placed perpendicular to the target line in order to ensure that the push from it will be parallel to the target line.

There should be a small time lag between the moment you start to transfer your weight back to your left side and the moment when your shoulders begin to unwind. When your shoulders begin to unwind, your hands will begin to pull on the club with a force that is parallel to the target line. The club will then be pulled parallel to the target line while the clubhead descends (see photograph **4.21**).

4.21

Pull on the club parallel to the target line as the clubhead descends back to the ball.

At every position on the arc along which the clubhead approaches the target line, it remains perpendicular to that arc. Your leg drive determines how quickly your shoulders unwind and how strongly your hands pull on the club. Continue to push from the right foot so that at the moment of impact your hips will have gone past being parallel to the target line. Your shoulders, however, will remain parallel to it. When your shoulders are parallel to the target line, your arms will move in the same direction, because they are attached to your shoulders. The clubface should be perpendicular to the ball and to the target line at the moment of impact because your shoulders and arms are in the correct position (see photograph **4.22**). Thus, no interference has been generated that will disrupt the position of your hands and clubface at the moment of impact.

This powerful exercise teaches you how to move the club through ninety degrees from behind the ball to parallel to the target line. I know of no better way of learning this than using the Paul Runyan set-up and hitting these little shots. The exercise also teaches you the reverse – how to move the club back to the ball through ninety degrees. To approach the ball from inside the target line and position the clubface perpendicular to the target line at the moment of impact, you need to be able to move the club in this manner.

This exercise also teaches you the importance of placing your right foot perpendicular to the target line. A right foot in that position transfers your weight back to the left side by directing a force parallel to the target line. This force causes the hips to unwind, which then causes the shoulders to unwind. When the shoulders unwind, the hands pull on the club with a force parallel to the target line.

4.22

At the moment of impact, with your shoulders parallel to the target line, your arms moving in the same direction as the target line, and the clubface perpendicular to the target line, you will apply a force to the ball in the direction of your target.

Once you can consistently position the club shaft parallel to the target line, and can apply maximum leg drive to these shots, start practising a fuller golf swing, using a bigger shoulder turn and cocking your wrists. To do this, modify the Paul Runyan set-up slightly, as described below. I use the modified Paul Runyan set-up to simulate my full swing, and coordinate the movement of my shoulders with the correct mechanics of my hand action.

Practise the modified Runyan set-up

1. Address the ball as you would when hitting stiff-wristed shots using the unmodified Runyan method described above.
2. Grip the club using the reverse overlapping grip, but this time, instead of having each palm facing upward at forty-five degrees, relax your wrists and grip the club with the palms facing each other, as in photograph **4.23**.

   When the palms face each other, the forearms no longer point upward. Continue to use the reverse overlapping grip and a bent left arm. Notice that I have also changed my stance by turning my left foot out by approximately twenty-two degrees. I do this because this time my swing will be very much like my regular full swing.
3. Begin your backswing by pushing the clubhead away from the ball with your left hand. By the time you have pushed the club to hip height it should be parallel to the target line, as usual.
4. Around hip height, as your shoulder turn continues, allow your wrists to cock in the way I described in Chapter 3, as in photograph **4.24**. Continue turning

4.23

Relax your wrists and change the position of your palms so that they face each other. If you wish, take your regular full swing stance, with the left foot turned out and the right foot perpendicular to the target line.

4.24

At hip height, add some cocking of the wrist to the modified Paul Runyan technique.

your shoulders, cocking your wrists, and transferring weight to your right side, as in photograph **4.25**.

5. When your back is facing your target, your shoulders are turned more or less ninety degrees, your left arm is bent, your weight is on your right side, and the club is positioned about three quarters of the way to the top of your usual backswing, begin transferring your weight to your left side to start your downswing; see photograph **4.26**.

It is critical to keep your left arm bent throughout this swing. Doing so seems

4.25

My shoulders are turning, I'm cocking my wrists, my left arm is bent, and I'm transferring my weight.

4.26

This is the top of the backswing for the modified Paul Runyan golf swing.

to focus your attention on the shoulders during the swing, not on the arms and hands, and thus produces accurate feedback concerning your shoulder turn, telling you what you need to know when you want to adjust it. Using the modified Paul Runyan golf swing is the simplest way I know of to monitor and adjust my shoulder turn so that my shoulders will be parallel to the target line at the moment of impact.

6. Continue to drive with your leg, and pull the club down the target line as your shoulders unwind. You can see in photograph **4.27** that the last three fingers of

4.27

Pull the butt of the club into the back of the ball with the shoulders parallel to the target.

my left hand are leading the movement of the club. To describe this, I like to say that I pull the butt of the club into the back of the ball. The Paul Runyan method of chipping and the modified version I am showing you here have one thing in common with the correct pivoting hand action of the golf swing – all three preserve the alignment of the sweet spots during the swing. Notice too that my shoulders are parallel to the target line.

As the downswing progresses, the club whips around the left thumb pad as the arms move parallel to the target line. Thus, at the moment of impact the left thumb pad returns to its original address position, with the clubface perpendicular to the target line, and a powerful force is directed to the ball, as in photograph **4.28**. The end result is a crisp shot that flies in the direction of your target.

4.28

When my shoulders are parallel to the target line and my arms are moving toward the target, my left thumb pad returns to its original address position and the clubface is perpendicular to the target line. These are the conditions that produce accurate, crisp golf shots.

Goodbye Until Next Time

I have shared with you my instructions concerning the hand action of the golf swing and how to coordinate the shoulder turn with this hand action. However, this book does not provide a detailed sequential description of the interactions that occur in the body and the hands during the backswing and the downswing.

I intend to write a follow-up book covering the interactions of the backswing and the downswing, as well as instructions on how the interactions of the full swing can be applied to your putting stroke. The principles of the putting stroke are simply the principles of the full swing adjusted for shortness of stroke.

My contribution to golf literature and golf instruction is only one small piece of the puzzle, but a significant one. The instructions in other golf books support the lessons given in this book, just as the instructions in this book support the lessons in other golf books. Take my advice: read as many golf books as you can.

Be patient with yourself and enjoy the journey. Goodbye until next time, and have fun!

Glossary

LIKE ALL GROUPS OF PEOPLE engaged in a specialized activity, golfers have evolved their own language. Although most of the language in this book will be self-explanatory, there are a few words that are used in ways that are peculiar to the golf world.

PLEASE NOTE: As in the text itself, the definitions were written as if they refer only to right-handed golfers, but of course they apply equally well to left-handed golfers when the appropriate adjustments are made.

Address position: the position one takes when preparing to hit the ball.

Blade iron: an iron that has a solid back and a smaller sweet spot than the cavity back iron (see below). Good shots are possible only if the ball is struck dead centre, on the smaller sweet spot.

Butt: the end of the club that the golfer grips.

Cavity back iron: an iron whose back is hollowed out to allow for perimeter weighting, which creates a larger sweet spot and thereby increases the possibility of hitting a good shot.

Chip: a shot that is played from just beside the green.

Closed address position: an address position in which the right foot, knee, hip, and shoulder are farther from the target line than the left foot, knee, hip, and shoulder; it produces a draw or a hook.

Closed clubface: from the point of view of the golfer in the address position, the clubface is "closed" when it is not perfectly perpendicular to the target line, because the toe of the clubface points slightly to the left.

Draw: a shot that at first moves to the right of the target line, and then gently flies back to the left; an experienced golfer will often hit a draw intentionally.

Fade: a shot that at first moves to the left of the target line and then gently flies back to the right; an experienced golfer will often hit a fade intentionally.

Flush: a shot will be "flush" when the relationship between the clubface and the ball is perfect at the moment of impact.

Grip down: to grip down is to place one's hands several inches closer to the clubhead than when one is hitting full shots.

Hook: a shot that at first moves well to the right of the target line, and then flies violently back to the left; usually unintentional.

Loft: the angle between the clubface and the ground; variations in loft produce variations in the height and distance of one's shots.

Open address position: an address position in which the right foot, knee, hip, and shoulder are closer to the target line than the left foot, knee, hip, and shoulder; it produces a fade or a slice.

Open clubface: from the point of view of the golfer in the address position, the clubface is "open" when it is not perfectly perpendicular to the target line, because the toe of the clubface points slightly to the right.

Slice: a shot that at first moves well to the left of the target line, and then flies violently back to the right; usually unintentional.

Sweet spots: the points on the ball and the clubface at which the two should make contact in order to achieve the desired result.

Takeaway: the initial twelve inches or so that the clubhead moves away from the ball at the beginning of the backswing.

The Parts of a Golf Club

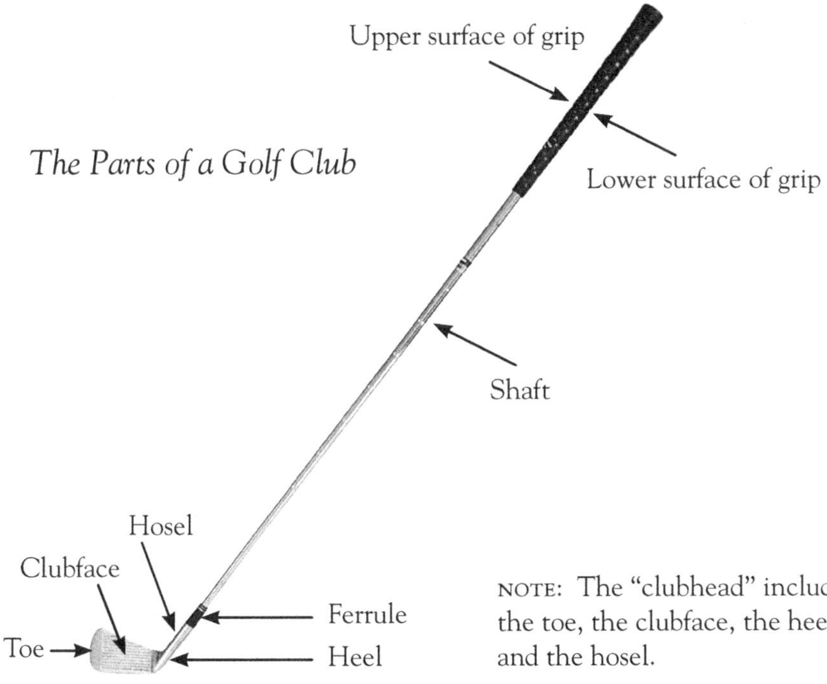

NOTE: The "clubhead" includes the toe, the clubface, the heel, and the hosel.

CPSIA information can be obtained at www.ICGtesting.com
Printed in the USA
LVOW02s1702171213

365739LV00009B/40/P

9 780991 924332